SERVING
San Antonio

A COOKBOOK FROM
ASSISTANCE LEAGUE® OF SAN ANTONIO

SERVING
San Antonio

A COOKBOOK FROM
ASSISTANCE LEAGUE® OF
SAN ANTONIO

A festive spirit comes alive along the

River Walk at night. Sounds of

laughter and conversation blend with the

music of mariachis and jazz combos.

Soft lights and enticing smells beckon

everyone to linger a little longer.

SERVING
San Antonio
A CULINARY AND CULTURAL MOSAIC
A COOKBOOK FROM ASSISTANCE LEAGUE® OF SAN ANTONIO

Library of Congress Control Number: 2006926573
ISBN-10: 0-9776944-0-2
ISBN-13: 978-0-9776944-0-2

Edited, designed and manufactured by
Favorite Recipes® Press
An imprint of

FRP™

P. O. Box 305142
Nashville, Tennessee 37230
800-358-0560

Art Director: Steve Newman
Book Design: Starletta Polster
Project Editor: Nicki Pendleton Wood

Manufactured in China
First Printing 2007   12,500 copies

DEDICATION

Serving San Antonio *is dedicated to all those who serve the diverse community of San Antonio.*

COOKBOOK COMMITTEE

Chairman—Cissi Glendening
Co-Chairman—Erin Byers

Underwriting Chairmen—K Joseph, Yvonne Kohutek
Underwriting Committee—Sue Staglik, Mary Stevenson

Recipe Chairman—Virginia Williamson
Recipe Section Chairman—Carmen Pettit

Recipe Committee
Jo Anne Herbold, Sally James, Anita Lindner, Donna Morton,
Audrey Oetting, Dianne Pool, Cheryl Tomandl

Non-recipe Text Chairmen—Jennie Martin, Mary Zuschlag

Distribution/Accounting Chairman—Marie Schmutz

Distribution Committee
Barbara Burleson, Phyllis Giffin, Carol Lapp, Ginger Nicholas,
Beth Roten, Betty Touchon, Carol Walters

Celebrity Chefs and Restaurant Chairman—Virna Reposa

Celebrity Chefs Committee
Shari Dybdahl, Marcia Lehman, Shirley Sweigart

Assistance League President 2006–2007 Dawne Wright

at&t

Edward E. Whitacre Jr.
Chairman and
Chief Executive Officer

175 E. Houston Street
San Antonio, TX 78205

T: 210.351.5400
F: 210.351.3553

Each year thousands of people come to San Antonio. They come to experience the multi-cultural offerings of food, architecture, music and people. There is a warmth about this big city that totally engulfs the soul. This is a city that cares about its people. Volunteers helping each other in the day-to-day process of living show this feeling through their many hours of service.

The Assistance League of San Antonio, with almost 500 dedicated members, provides thousands of hours of service each year through its various projects. <u>Serving San Antonio</u> invites each of you to experience the food and the history surrounding this special city. It offers the opportunity, through its purchase, to expand the philanthropic projects serving San Antonio. Enjoy the city, enjoy the culture, enjoy the music, but especially enjoy the feeling of satisfaction you get knowing you helped someone in need.

Thank you for supporting this organization, and I hope you enjoy this cookbook.

Ed Whitacre

CITY OF SAN ANTONIO
PHIL HARDBERGER
MAYOR

Greetings!

Service is at the heart of our city. Missionaries and early settlers understood that community strength is based upon service. Today, the great strength of San Antonio is still the service provided by its volunteer, civic, religious and military organizations. Our great city is blessed with numerous philanthropic groups which have pledged their time and resources to help people in need.

The members of the Assistance League of San Antonio have demonstrated an exemplary record by identifying under-served areas of need and providing daily acts of service designed to improve the welfare of our community's citizens, both young and old. In this detailed cookbook you will not only learn about the projects of Assistance League, but you will also have the opportunity to discover the culinary and cultural mosaic that is San Antonio. I hope you enjoy it.

Sincerely,

Phil Hardberger

Phil Hardberger
Mayor

Serving San Antonio
COOKBOOK PARTNERS

TEXAS STAR

Front Cover Sponsor—Weston Solutions

Back Cover Sponsor—AT&T Foundation

FIESTA PATRON
Photography Sponsors

K & Tom Joseph

Diane & John Leininger
Mercy International

Anonymous donor

BLUEBONNET
Sidebar Sponsors

Bar K Ranch
Kohutek Beefmasters, Victoria, Texas

Bjorn's Audio•Video•Home Theater

INDIAN PAINTBRUSH

Erin & Brent Byers

M E Salon and Spa

Raba-Kistner

Wells Fargo San Antonio
Commercial Banking

PRIMROSE

Broadway National Bank

Grady's BarBQ Restaurants

YELLOW ROSE

The Charitable Foundation of
Frost National Bank

Connolly & Company
Public relations, advertising, marketing

Intercontinental National Bank

In Honor of Las Palomas Class

Kenneth L. Logsdon

Pizza Hut of San Antonio

Mr. & Mrs. Graham Weston

ACKNOWLEDGMENTS

The Antique Rose Emporium

Pam & Art Burdick, Burdick Homes

Tommy Dismuke,
San Antonio Flower Company

Chef Michael Flores,
Learn Aboard! Cooking Class

The Guenther House

Edali Hernandez, Los Pueblitas,
El Mercado

The Lodge Restaurant of Castle Hills

Rio San Antonio River Cruises, Inc.

San Antonio Botanical Garden Center

CONTACT DETAILS

AT&T Foundation
120 Travis Street, Suite 350
San Antonio, TX 78205

Bar K Ranch
Kohutek Beefmasters
Victoria County

Bjorn's Audio • Video • Home Theater
14123 Highway 281 North
San Antonio, TX 78259

Erin & Brent Byers

Connolly & Company Ltd
7373 Broadway, Suite 109
San Antonio, TX 78209

The Charitable Foundation of
Frost National Bank
P. O. Box 1600
San Antonio, TX 78296

Grady's Bar-B-Q Restaurants
P. O. Box 13430
San Antonio, TX 78213

Intercontinental National Bank
6820 Military Drive West
San Antonio, TX 78227

Tom & K Joseph
900 NE Loop 410
San Antonio, TX 78209

Las Palomas Class
Anonymous Donor

Kenneth Logsdon
Wachovia Securities
Spring, TX

Diane & John Leininger
Mercy International

M E Salon and Spa
21215 West Tejas Trail
San Antonio, TX 78257

Raba-Kistner Consultants, Inc.
12821 West Golden Lane
San Antonio,TX 78249

Mr. & Mrs. Graham Weston
112 East Pecan Street, Box 6
San Antonio, TX 78205

Wells Fargo San Antonio
Commercial Banking
16414 San Pedro Avenue
San Antonio, TX 78232-2277

Weston Solutions
70 NE Loop 410
San Antonio, TX 78216

PREFACE

What do you get when you bring together more than 470 women with the common goal of providing assistance to residents of the San Antonio area regardless of race, creed, or religious affiliation? You get Assistance League® of San Antonio, an organization dedicated to promoting self-esteem, achievement, and education within the local community. In addition, you get a diverse source of wonderful recipes that have been shared by chapter members at their meetings, luncheons, teas, and dinners.

Assistance League of San Antonio was founded as a guild in 1984 and was chartered as the 76th Chapter of National Assistance League in 1988. This 501(c)(3) nonprofit organization has no paid employees. Additionally, the chapter's Auxiliary, Bexar Hugs, certified in 1995, offers serving opportunities for women who are not able to volunteer on weekdays.

All money raised by Assistance League is used to fund its local philanthropic projects. The organization's main fund-raiser is its Thrift House, located at 2611 West Avenue. Other funding sources include an annual "Treasures at Twilight" gala, grants, donations, memorials, and bequests from family and friends. This cookbook is the chapter's most recent fund-raiser.

Assistance League's philanthropic projects are serviced through agencies, schools, and organizations that verify actual needs of individuals. Whether the members of Assistance League are working on a project, a fund-raiser, or a recipe to share, they have a common goal of SERVING with a purpose.

Our hope is that with each discovery of a special recipe that brings you joy and satisfaction, you will think about the lives that are being touched through proceeds from this cookbook.

Imagine the pride of college students when a scholarship allows them to complete their degrees or the relief of indigent mothers when they are given clothing and other essentials for their newborn babies and preschoolers. Consider how the lives of children are changed when their parents learn basic developmental and health information. Reflect on the joy experienced by assisted-living residents who are visited on a regular basis by Assistance League friends. Picture classrooms of inquisitive students as they learn personal safety during interactive presentations and busloads of excited children as they take home the new clothes that they have personally selected. Envision the delight of acutely ill children as they choose hand-decorated ball caps.

More information about how Assistance League is "Serving San Antonio" can be found on the introductory pages of each section. The enjoyment this cookbook brings you is only the beginning of its impact.

CONTENTS

APPEALING APPETIZERS & BEVERAGES

NOW SERVING:
THE MISSING INGREDIENT

Have you ever had the desire, time and enthusiasm to make a favorite appetizer but were stopped short of your goal because you didn't have an essential ingredient? This frustrating experience is similar to one many college students face. Their missing ingredient is the money to complete their degrees.

Each spring junior and senior college students enrolled in a four-year program in the San Antonio area can apply for **College Scholarships** awarded by Assistance League® of San Antonio. More scholarship information is available on the chapter's Web site, www.alsanantonio.org.

AFTERNOON BRIDAL TEA

Shrimp Mold page 26
Feta Pine Nut Spread with Assorted Crackers page 27
Ham and Cheese Rolls page 81
Cucumber Sandwiches
Sweetwater Strawberry Shortbread page 90
"President's Tea" Iced Coffee page 28
Champagne

BLUE CHEESE-STUFFED MUSHROOMS

3 pounds large mushrooms
(about 40)
1 cup chopped green onions
6 tablespoons butter
8 ounces blue cheese, crumbled
1/4 teaspoon salt
1/4 teaspoon pepper
2 teaspoons Tabasco sauce
1/2 to 3/4 cup bread crumbs
10 tablespoons butter

Carefully remove the stems from the mushrooms. Mince the stems in a food processor with a steel blade. Sauté the minced stems and green onions in 6 tablespoons butter in a large skillet until tender. Add the blue cheese and cook until melted, stirring constantly. Some lumps may remain. Stir in the salt, pepper and Tabasco sauce. Add the bread crumbs and mix until of stuffing consistency. Sauté the mushroom caps in 10 tablespoons butter; cool. Spoon in the stuffing mixture. Arrange on a baking sheet and bake in a preheated 425-degree oven until heated through.

MAKES 40 SERVINGS

BLUE CHEESE "FROSTED" PEARS

4 ounces blue cheese, crumbled
1/2 cup (1 stick) butter,
softened
1 cup chopped pecans or walnuts
Several firm pears

Combine the cheese and butter in a medium bowl until thoroughly blended. Spread the pecans on a plate or waxed paper. Cut pears into quarters and remove cores and seeds. Spread the blue cheese mixture on all sides of the large end of each pear quarter. Roll in the pecans, pressing them into the cheese mixture.

MAKES VARIABLE SERVINGS

Select Bartlett or Bosc pears for this recipe because they hold their shape and provide a unique taste.

SALSA-BAKED GOAT CHEESE

Arrange the cornhusks slightly overlapping in the bottom of a small baking dish or individual tapas dishes.

Toast the pine nuts on a baking sheet or in a dry skillet for 5 minutes or until brown and fragrant. Combine with the goat cheese and cream cheese in a medium bowl and mix well.

Divide the cheese mixture in half. Shape each half into a disk. Arrange one disk on two cornhusks. Surround with half the salsa. Fold the cornhusks over to enclose the cheese disk and salsa. Tie with kitchen string. Repeat with the remaining cheese disk and cornhusks.

Bake in a preheated 350-degree oven for 10 to 15 minutes or until heated through. Cut the string and open the cornhusks. Sprinkle with the cilantro. Serve with chips, crackers or toasted focaccia.

To make one large appetizer, arrange the cornhusks slightly overlapping in a large baking dish. Pat the cheese into a disk on the cornhusks and surround with the salsa. Fold the cornhusks over to enclose the cheese disk and salsa. Tie with kitchen string. Proceed as directed above.

Cornhusks can be found in the Mexican food section of most supermarkets.

MAKES 4 TO 6 SERVINGS

4 cornhusks, soaked in
water overnight
1/4 cup pine nuts or coarsely
ground pecans
4 ounces soft goat cheese (chèvre)
4 ounces cream cheese, softened
1 cup good-quality salsa
1 tablespoon chopped
fresh cilantro

WON TONS HAWAIIAN STYLE

1 (8-ounce) can water chestnuts

1 (8-ounce) can bamboo shoots

2 carrots, peeled

1 small onion

4 garlic cloves

1 piece fresh ginger

2 ribs celery

1 1/2 pounds ground pork

1 1/2 pounds ground beef

1/2 cup oyster sauce

Salt and pepper to taste

100 small won ton wrappers

1 egg, beaten

Combine the water chestnuts, bamboo shoots, carrots, onion, garlic, ginger and celery in a food processor. Process until minced. Combine with the pork and beef in a bowl. Add the oyster sauce, salt and pepper and mix well. Chill for 30 minutes. Brush half of each wrap with the egg. Spoon about 1/2 teaspoon of the filling on the wrap. Fold the wrap over the filling and press the edges to seal. Repeat with the remaining filling and wraps. Fry the won tons in hot oil in a deep pan until golden brown.

MAKES ABOUT 100

FAMOUS LETTUCE WRAPS

2 chicken breasts

2 tablespoons vegetable oil

2/3 cup canned straw mushrooms
or other mushrooms, chopped

1 cup minced water chestnuts

3 tablespoons chopped
green onions

1 garlic clove, minced

2 tablespoons soy sauce

2 tablespoons dark brown sugar

1 teaspoon rice vinegar

1 tablespoon vegetable oil

1 head iceberg lettuce

Sauté the chicken breasts in 2 tablespoons hot oil in a skillet over medium heat until cooked through. Cool slightly and chop. Mix mushrooms, water chestnuts, green onions and garlic in a bowl. Combine the soy sauce, brown sugar and rice vinegar in a small bowl. Heat 1 tablespoon oil in the skillet over low heat. Warm the chicken and mushroom mixture in the oil. Stir in the soy sauce mixture. Cut the lettuce into halves and remove lettuce "cups." Scoop some of the chicken mixture into the individual lettuce cups. Roll to enclose the filling.

MAKES 4 TO 6 SERVINGS

BLUE CHEESE CRUMBLE

Sprinkle the cheese into a shallow 6- or 8-inch dish. Combine the garlic and olive oil in a small bowl and drizzle over the cheese. Combine the vinegar, lemon juice, parsley and onion in a small bowl and pour over the cheese. Chill for 1 hour. Sprinkle with pepper. Serve with Fuji apple slices and wheat crackers.

MAKES 8 TO 10 SERVINGS

8 ounces blue cheese, crumbled
2 garlic cloves, mashed
1/3 cup olive oil
3 tablespoons red wine vinegar
1 tablespoon lemon juice
1/2 cup chopped parsley
1/2 cup chopped red onion
Freshly ground black pepper to taste

CHILE CON QUESO Y CARNE

Brown the ground beef and sausage in a large Dutch oven over medium heat, stirring until crumbly. Add the onion and cook until tender; drain. Stir in the tomatoes with green chiles, green chiles and pepper. Reduce the heat to low and add the cheeses. Cook until melted, stirring constantly. Simmer for 30 minutes, stirring frequently. Serve with tortilla chips.

MAKES 20 TO 30 SERVINGS

1 pound ground round
1 pound Jimmy Dean
   hot sausage
1 onion, chopped
1 (10-ounce) can tomatoes with
   green chiles, drained
1 (4-ounce) can diced green chiles
Dash of pepper
1 pound medium Cheddar
   cheese, cubed
2 pounds Velveeta cheese, cubed

When the Spanish permanently settled in the San Antonio area, they constructed seven acequias (irrigation ditches) to supply nearby farmlands with water from the San Antonio River and San Pedro Creek. The acequias were San Antonio's only water system for two hundred years, and they are still serving the city today.

CAPONATA

1 eggplant
(about 1 pound), peeled and
cut into 1/2-inch pieces
1 (14-ounce) can diced
Italian tomatoes
1 onion, chopped
1 red bell pepper,
cut into 1/2-inch pieces
1/2 cup medium-hot salsa
1/4 cup olive oil
2 tablespoons capers, drained
2 tablespoons balsamic vinegar
3 garlic cloves, minced
1 teaspoon dried oregano
1/4 teaspoon salt
1/3 cup sliced fresh basil

Combine the eggplant, tomatoes, onion, bell pepper, salsa, olive oil, capers, vinegar, garlic, oregano and salt in a slow cooker and mix well. Cook on Low for 7 to 8 hours. Stir in the basil. Serve the mixture at room temperature with toasted French bread.

MAKES 10 TO 12 SERVINGS

Bell peppers are the sweet-fleshed members of the pepper family. Green bell peppers ripen into the red and yellow varieties. The ripened peppers have a sweeter flavor.

SINFUL SPUDS

Cut a thin slice from the top and the bottom of each potato. Cut the potatoes into halves crosswise. Combine with the water and kosher salt in a large saucepan over high heat. Bring to a boil. Reduce the heat and let simmer for 10 to 15 minutes or until the potatoes are tender; do not overcook. Drain and cool.

Crumble the cheese in a small bowl with a fork. Add the pine nuts, green olives, olive oil, currants, lemon zest, oregano and pepper and mix well.

Scoop out the center of each potato with a spoon or melon baller and discard. Fill the center with a heaping teaspoon of the cheese mixture. Garnish with a parsley leaf.

MAKES 24 SERVINGS

12 small new potatoes, uniform
   in size and shape
6 cups water
1 1/2 teaspoons kosher salt
1/2 cup feta cheese
1/4 cup pine nuts, toasted
2 tablespoons chopped
   green olives
1 tablespoon extra-virgin
   olive oil
1 tablespoon dried currants
1/2 teaspoon chopped lemon zest
1/4 teaspoon oregano
1/4 teaspoon pepper

The feta mixture, without the pine nuts, can be prepared up to two days in advance and refrigerated. Let the mixture stand at room temperature for 1 hour before using. Stir in the pine nuts when you're ready to stuff the potatoes. The potatoes can be stuffed up to four hours before serving. Feta cheese is sometimes referred to as pickled cheese. It provides a robust, savory flavor to appetizers, salads, and cooked dishes.

WILLIAMSBURG CHEESE STRAWS

1 cup sifted all-purpose flour
1/2 teaspoon salt
1/4 teaspoon dry mustard
1/8 teaspoon cayenne pepper
1/3 cup butter, softened
1/2 cup (2 ounces) shredded
extra-sharp Cheddar cheese
1 1/2 tablespoons ice water
1/2 cup (2 ounces) shredded
extra-sharp Cheddar cheese
1 teaspoon celery seeds

Sift the flour, salt, dry mustard and cayenne pepper into a medium bowl. Cut in the butter and 1/2 cup cheese with a pastry blender until the mixture is crumbly. Add the ice water and stir to blend. Shape the mixture into a ball.

Roll on a lightly floured surface to 1/8-inch thickness. Sprinkle with the remaining cheese. Fold the dough in half and roll again to 1/8-inch thickness. Cut into 1/2×3-inch pieces with a knife or pastry wheel. Sprinkle with the celery seeds. Arrange on an ungreased baking sheet and bake in a preheated 350-degree oven for 12 minutes or until light brown. Serve warm or cool. May be frozen and reheated in a slow oven.

MAKES 60 SERVINGS

QUICK SAUSAGE SLICES

1 pound Italian sausage,
casings removed
2/3 cup shredded
mozzarella cheese
1/2 cup sour cream
6 tablespoons mayonnaise
1/4 cup chopped green onions
1 teaspoon Worcestershire sauce
2 loaves French bread,
cut into slices

Brown the sausage in a skillet, stirring until crumbly; drain. Combine with the cheese, sour cream, mayonnaise, green onions and Worcestershire sauce in a medium bowl and mix well. Spread a small amount of the mixture on each bread slice. Arrange on a baking sheet. Broil until the topping melts, taking care not to burn the edges. Serve hot.

MAKES ABOUT 20 SERVINGS

VEGETABLE SQUARES

Press the rolls into a 9×13-inch pan, pressing the seams to seal. Bake in a preheated 350-degree oven until light brown. Cool completely.

Combine the cream cheese and dressing mix in a bowl and mix well. Spread over the cooled crust. Toss the vegetables in a bowl to combine and spread over the cream cheese mixture. Top with the Cheddar cheese. Bake in a preheated 350-degree oven just until the cheese melts. Cool and cut into squares. Serve warm or cold.

MAKES 24 SERVINGS

1 (8- to 10-ounce) can refrigerator crescent rolls
8 ounces cream cheese, softened
1 envelope ranch dressing mix
1/4 cup chopped carrots
1/4 cup chopped cauliflower
1/4 cup chopped broccoli
1/4 cup chopped mushrooms
1/4 cup chopped green onions
1 cup (4 ounces) shredded Cheddar cheese

ARTICHOKE SPREAD

Combine the artichokes, green chiles, cheese and mayonnaise in a large bowl and mix well. Spread the mixture in a glass baking dish. Bake in a preheated 350-degree oven for 20 minutes. Serve with crackers or toasted baguette slices.

MAKES 6 TO 8 SERVINGS

1 (15-ounce) can artichokes, drained, squeezed dry and chopped
1 (4-ounce) can chopped green chiles
1 cup mayonnaise
1 cup (4 ounces) Parmesan cheese

In 1691, on their way to visit missions in East Texas, Spanish priests stopped to celebrate the feast day of Saint Anthony de Padua in an area that is now known as San Antonio.

21

PESTO CHEESE BLOSSOM

8 ounces provolone cheese, sliced

16 ounces cream cheese, softened

20 pistachios, shelled

2 garlic cloves

1/2 cup fresh basil leaves

1/2 cup fresh parsley leaves

1/2 cup pine nuts

1/4 teaspoon salt

1/4 teaspoon freshly
ground pepper

2 tablespoons extra-virgin
olive oil

3 ounces oil-pack
sun-dried tomatoes

This appetizer is a great one to prepare in advance. It makes a beautiful presentation, providing deliciously intense flavors.

Line a medium bowl with plastic wrap, leaving enough overhang to cover the top. Reserve 3 slices of the provolone cheese. Line the bottom and side of the bowl with the remaining provolone cheese, overlapping the slices.

Process the cream cheese, pistachios and 1 garlic clove in a food processor until well blended. Spoon into a bowl.

Combine the remaining garlic clove, basil, parsley and pine nuts in a food processor and process until well blended. Combine the salt, pepper and olive oil in a bowl and mix well. With the food processor running, add the olive oil mixture in a thin stream. Spoon into a bowl.

Drain the tomatoes, reserving the oil. Purée the tomatoes with a small amount of the oil.

Spread some of the cream cheese mixture over the provolone cheese slices in the bowl. Layer with the pesto mixture, half the remaining cream cheese and the tomato mixture. Top with the remaining cream cheese mixture and cover with the reserved provolone cheese. Bring the edges of the plastic wrap together over the top and secure with a twist tie.

Chill until firm. Remove the plastic wrap and invert the blossom onto a serving platter. Garnish with fresh basil, parsley or strips of sun-dried tomato. Serve with party crackers. The blossom will keep in the refrigerator for to 2 weeks.

MAKES 12 TO 15 SERVINGS

L.B.'S GREEN CHILE DIP

Mix the cream cheese and sour cream in a bowl until well blended. Stir in the green chiles, pepperoni, chives and green onions. Spoon into a baking dish. Top with the pecans. Bake in a preheated 350-degree oven for 20 minutes or until bubbly. Serve with scoop-shaped corn chips.

MAKES 8 SERVINGS

8 ounces cream cheese, softened

1/2 cup sour cream

1 (4-ounce) can chopped
   green chiles

1 (6-ounce) package
   pepperoni, chopped

3 tablespoons chives

1 1/2 tablespoons chopped
   green onions

1/2 cup chopped pecans

SIX-LAYER BOMBAY CHEESE

Combine the cream cheese, Cheddar cheese and curry powder in a bowl with a spoon until smooth. Shape into a 5-inch disk on a serving plate. Chill, covered, for 45 minutes or until firm.

Spread the chutney over the cheese mixture. Sprinkle with the pecans and onion. Arrange crackers around the cheese mixture and serve.

MAKES 6 TO 8 SERVINGS

8 ounces cream cheese, softened

4 ounces sharp Cheddar
   cheese, shredded

1/2 teaspoon curry powder

1/2 (8-ounce) jar chutney

1/4 cup toasted pecans

1 generous tablespoon chopped
   green onion

The cheese can be prepared up to 2 days in advance. Cover and chill. The platter can be prepared up to an hour before serving and kept cool.

23

GARLIC SHRIMP

24 large fresh shrimp
1/2 cup olive oil
1/4 cup chopped fresh parsley
3 garlic cloves, minced
1/2 teaspoon red pepper flakes
1/4 teaspoon black pepper
1/4 cup (1/2 stick) butter, melted
(or olive oil)
1/2 cup herb-seasoned bread crumbs
1/2 cup (2 ounces) freshly grated
Parmesan cheese

Peel and devein the shrimp. Arrange in a 7×11-inch baking dish. Pour the olive oil over the shrimp. Combine the parsley, garlic, pepper flakes and black pepper in a small bowl. Sprinkle over the shrimp. Bake, covered, in a preheated 300-degree oven for 15 minutes. Turn the shrimp over and drizzle with the butter. Sprinkle with the bread crumbs and cheese. Bake, uncovered, for 5 to 10 minutes longer or until the shrimp are cooked through.

MAKES 2 SERVINGS

CILANTRO MOUSSE

5 serrano chiles
1 bunch cilantro, stems removed
1/2 small yellow onion
8 ounces cream cheese, softened
1 cup mayonnaise
1/2 cup milk
1 tablespoon chicken
bouillon granules
1/2 cup hot water
2 envelopes unflavored gelatin

Remove the seeds from 2 of the serrano chiles. Process the cilantro, serrano chiles and onion in a food processor until well blended, scraping down the sides. Add the cream cheese and pulse for 1 minute. Add the mayonnaise and process to blend. Drizzle the milk into the food processor with the motor running. Dissolve the bouillon granules in the hot water. Stir in the gelatin until well combined. Drizzle into the food processor with the motor running. Pour the mixture into a 4-cup ring mold coated with nonstick cooking spray. Chill until set. Unmold onto a serving dish. Fill the center with parsley sprigs. Serve with crackers.

MAKES 12 SERVINGS

CRAB IMPERIAL

Sauté the celery and bell pepper in the butter in a skillet until tender. Combine the parsley, Old Bay seasoning, dry mustard, red pepper, hot pepper sauce, mayonnaise, egg and crab meat in a bowl and mix well. Add the sautéed mixture and mix well. Spoon into a small greased baking dish. Bake in a peheated 375-degree oven for 15 minutes or until heated through and bubbly. Serve hot with crackers.

MAKES 8 TO 10 SERVINGS

2 small ribs celery, chopped
1/2 small green bell
*   pepper, chopped*
1 tablespoon butter
1 tablespoon chopped
*   fresh parsley*
1 teaspoon Old Bay seasoning
1/2 teaspoon dry mustard
1/8 teaspoon red pepper
1/8 teaspoon hot red pepper sauce
3 tablespoons mayonnaise
1 egg
1 pound fresh lump crab meat,
*   drained and flaked*

CRAWFISH ELEGANTE

Sauté the crawfish tails in 1/4 cup butter in a skillet for about 10 minutes and set aside. Sauté the green onions and parsley in 1/2 cup butter in another skillet. Add the flour and mix well. Add the half-and-half. Cook until the sauce thickens, stirring constantly. Stir in the sherry. Drain the crawfish and add to the sauce. Season with salt, pepper and cayenne pepper. Serve hot with crackers.

MAKES 8 TO 10 SERVINGS

1 pound crawfish tails
1/4 cup (1/2 stick) butter
1 large bunch green
*   onions, chopped*
2 tablespoons chopped parsley
1/2 cup (1 stick) butter
3 tablespoons all-purpose flour
1 pint half-and-half
3 tablespoons sherry
Salt and pepper to taste
Dash of cayenne pepper

SHRIMP MOLD

1 cup prepared tomato soup
1 envelope unflavored gelatin
1/4 cup cold water
8 ounces cream cheese, softened
1 cup mayonnaise
1 (6-ounce) can crab meat
1 cup cooked small shrimp,
chopped if needed
1/2 cup chopped onion
1/2 cup chopped celery
1/2 cup chopped green bell pepper

Heat the soup to boiling in a saucepan. Soften the gelatin in the cold water. Add to the soup and mix well.

Beat the cream cheese and mayonnaise in a bowl until well blended. Add to the soup mixture and mix well. Stir in the crab meat, shrimp, onion, celery and bell pepper. Pour the mixture into a greased 6-cup gelatin mold. Chill until firm. Umold onto a serving platter and serve with crackers.

MAKES 12 SERVINGS

MEXICORN DIP

2 (15-ounce) cans fiesta
corn, drained
1 cup mayonnaise
1 cup sour cream
1 tablespoon sugar
1 (4-ounce) can chopped
green chiles
8 ounces shredded sharp
Cheddar cheese
1 or 2 jalapeño chiles, chopped
3 or 4 green onions, chopped

Combine the corn, mayonnaise, sour cream, sugar, green chiles, cheese, jalapeño chiles and green onions in a medium bowl and mix well. Chill for several hours for the flavors to blend. Dust the top with a small amount of chili powder or paprika to garnish. Serve with scoop-shaped corn chips.

MAKES 7 TO 8 CUPS

FETA PINE NUT SPREAD

Combine the cream cheese spread, yogurt, pine nuts, basil and garlic in a food processor. Pulse until well combined. Add the cheese and tomatoes and pulse until combined but still chunky. Spoon the spread into a serving bowl and serve with crackers. (Can be made up to 3 days ahead and stored, covered, in the refrigerator.)

MAKES 2 CUPS

1 (8-ounce) tub whipped cream cheese spread
1/2 cup plain nonfat yogurt
3 tablespoons toasted pine nuts
2 tablespoons packed chopped fresh basil
1 garlic clove, minced
7 ounces feta cheese, crumbled
1/3 cup chopped drained oil-pack sun-dried tomatoes

PECAN CRANBERRY SPREAD

Beat the cream cheese with an electric mixer until soft and fluffy. Spoon into a small bowl. Stir in the pecans, cranberries and orange juice concentrate. Chill, covered, for 30 minutes for the flavors to blend. Serve with plain crackers, quick bread or tea loaf.

MAKES 1 CUP

4 ounces cream cheese, softened
1 1/4 cups chopped pecans, toasted
1/4 cup dried cranberries
2 tablespoons orange juice concentrate

27

"PRESIDENT'S TEA" ICED COFFEE

1 quart hot water
1/4 cup instant coffee granules
2 cups sugar
1 small can chocolate syrup
2 quarts cold water
2 quarts milk
1 gallon vanilla ice cream

Combine the hot water and coffee granules in a container and mix well. Stir in the sugar, chocolate syrup and cold water. Chill in the refrigerator overnight. Add the milk and ice cream just before serving.

MAKES 32 SERVINGS

COFFEE DELIGHT

1 quart coffee ice cream
1 cup milk
1 1/2 cups bourbon
1/4 cup light rum
1/4 cup crème de cacao

Combine the ice cream, milk, bourbon, rum and crème de cacao in a blender. Process until well blended. Serve in wine glasses or brandy snifters for an after-dinner treat.

MAKES 4 TO 8 SERVINGS

Rum, cognac and other distilled flavors are best used in beverages or dishes that are not heated to maintain their character.

MARKET SQUARE/EL MERCADO

*Located within two blocks of the River Walk, Market Square was developed
in 1840 as a town market, a service it still performs today.
Market Square surrounds El Mercado, an indoor shopping center offering
an authentic sampling of Mexican culture, crafts, and cuisine.
Restaurants and additional shops can be found in Market Square, where one
can leisurely stroll while listening to the melodic tunes of mariachis.*

PARADISE COOLER

2 quarts orange juice, chilled
2 (46-ounce) cans unsweetened
pineapple juice, chilled
2 (6-ounce) cans frozen
limeade concentrate
2 (28-ounce) bottles lemon-lime
soda or ginger ale

Combine the orange juice, pineapple juice and limeade concentrate in a large cooler or punch bowl. Add the soda just before serving. Pour over ice and garnish with lime slices and strawberry halves.

MAKES 50 SERVINGS

MARGARITA FOR ONE

1 slice lime
Coarse or kosher salt
1/2 ounce fresh lime juice
1 1/2 ounces tequila
1/2 ounce Triple Sec
3 or 4 ice cubes

Rub the inside rim of a chilled 4-ounce tumbler or cocktail glass with the lime. Pour salt into a saucer. Invert the tumbler onto the salt to thinly coat the rim.

Combine the lime juice, tequila, Triple Sec and ice cubes in a shaker. Shake vigorously 9 or 10 times to blend. Strain into the salted glass.

For a frozen margarita, combine the lime juice, tequila, Triple Sec and ice cubes in a blender and process until slushy.

MAKES 1 SERVING

PUNCHY SANGRIA

Combine the lemonade, wine, lime juice and club soda in a large pitcher or punch bowl. Cut the lemon and orange into slices and float on the punch. Serve over ice.

MAKES 10 CUPS

2 (6-ounce) cans frozen pink lemonade, thawed

4 1/2 cups rosé, chilled

Juice of 1 lime

2 cups chilled club soda

1 lemon

1 orange

WHITE SANGRIA

Pour the riesling and vino verde into a large pitcher. Cut the pear, apple, lime and lemon half into thin slices. Add to the pitcher. Stir in the Grand Marnier and sugar. Let stand for several hours or refrigerate overnight. Fill the pitcher with ice cubes and add the ginger ale to serve.

MAKES 4 TO 5 SERVINGS

1 (750-milliliter) bottle riesling

1 (750-milliliter) bottle vino verde

1 firm pear, rinsed

1 Granny Smith apple, rinsed

1 lime, rinsed

1/2 lemon, rinsed

6 tablespoons Grand Marnier

3 to 4 tablespoons sugar

12 ounces ginger ale or grapefruit soda

Sangria, usually made with red wine, is a delicious and refreshing drink served as a complement to spicy Mexican food by San Antonians. It also goes well with flavorful appetizers and grilled appetizers.

31

COSMOPOLITAN SÍ! SÍ!

2 ounces citrus-flavored vodka

1/2 ounce Cointreau

2 to 3 ounces cranberry juice

Juice of 1/4 to 1/2 fresh lime

Combine the vodka, Cointreau, cranberry juice and lime juice with a generous amount of ice in a cocktail shaker. Shake vigorously to blend. Strain into a martini glass.

MAKES 1 SERVING

SADIE THOMPSON (OR MISSIONARY'S DOWNFALL)

1 ounce crushed pineapple, or

1 slice fresh pineapple

2 ounces pineapple juice

1 1/2 ounces Puerto Rican rum

1 ounce cherry brandy

3 ounces crushed ice

Combine the pineapple, pineapple juice, rum, brandy and ice in a blender. Process until slushy. Serve in a cocktail glass. Garnish with a small wedge of pineapple.

MAKES 1 SERVING

As Mammy's Shanty says:
"The rains came and, Brother, how it rained!
Then Sadie came; then Brother Davidson
came, and it still rained, and the sky wept.
There was water, water, everywhere, and too much
of it to drink. But Sadie quickly remedied this
water hazard by mixing a tropical brew of herbs and
fruit juices, and some native spirits, which, plus
Sadie's charm, led to Brother Davidson's downfall.
And the rains came. . .and who cared?"

SPICY TOMATO WARM-UP

Combine the vegetable juice cocktail, bouillon, lemon juice, Worcestershire sauce, pepper and hot pepper sauce in a saucepan. Heat until the bouillon cubes dissolve, stirring constantly. Serve warm in mugs or Irish coffee glasses.

MAKES ABOUT 5 1/2 CUPS

1 (46-ounce) can spicy vegetable
  juice cocktail
3 beef bouillon cubes
3 tablespoons lemon juice
1 tablespoon Worcestershire sauce
1/8 teaspoon pepper
1/4 to 1/2 teaspoon hot red
  pepper sauce

WASSAIL

Combine the sugar, water, cinnamon sticks and lemon in a medium saucepan. Bring to a boil and cook for 5 minutes, stirring constantly.

Combine the pineapple juice, orange juice, sauterne and sherry in a Dutch oven. Bring to a boil, then simmer, covered, for 10 minutes. Stir in the sugar syrup and heat thoroughly. Remove the lemon slices and cinnamon sticks. Garnish each serving with a pineapple wedge.

MAKES 3 1/2 QUARTS

2 1/2 cups sugar
1 cup water
8 (3-inch) cinnamon sticks
1 lemon, sliced
1 quart pineapple juice
1 quart orange juice
5 cups sauterne
1/2 cup dry sherry
1/2 cup lemon juice

"Wassail," an Old English term, means "be in good health." Originally, wassail recipes used mulled beer, and later on, cider.

BOUNTIFUL BREAKFASTS, BRUNCHES & BREADS

NOW SERVING: A SUBSTANTIAL START

What you eat for breakfast can affect the rest of your day. A breakfast with sufficient energy resources provides your body with a helpful start to meet the day's challenges. Some children begin their lives without the basic resources they need. The **Togs for Tots** project gives these children a helpful start by providing newborns through preschool-age children with new clothing, personal care items, and picture books. Premature infants are also given developmental toys. Caregivers receive a booklet of important developmental, nutritional, and immunization information.

Community agencies identify the children and deliver the items to them. While most of the clothes are purchased by volunteer buyers, gowns for newborns are sewn by Assistance League® members. Filling agency requests is a year-round activity that is done by a group of volunteers who seek to serve those in need.

HOLIDAY BRUNCH	FIESTA BRUNCH
Bloody Marys or Mimosas	*Cilantro Mousse* page 24
Pecan Cranberry Spread page 27	*Chile con Queso y Carne with*
Cream Cheese	*Assorted Crackers and Tortilla Chips* page 17
Toast Points	*Green Chile Egg Casserole* page 44
Oven-Glazed Bacon page 36	*Crisp Bacon and Sausage Links*
Overnight French Toast page 37	*Jicama Slaw* page 67
Orange Pecan Scones page 86	*Mexican Rice* page 113
Orange and Candied Almond Salad page 61	*Corn Pudding* page 99
Festive Cranberry Torte page 149	*Crème Caramel (Flan)* page 148
Eggnog and Coffee	*Margaritas and Coffee*

OVEN-GLAZED BACON

8 ounces bacon
1/2 cup packed brown sugar
1 teaspoon Dijon mustard
2 tablespoons red wine vinegar

Arrange the bacon on a baking sheet and bake in a preheated 350-degree oven until almost crisp; drain. Combine the brown sugar, Dijon mustard and vinegar in a small bowl. Brush half over the bacon. Bake for 10 minutes longer. Turn the bacon and drizzle with the remaining sugar mixture. Bake for 10 minutes longer. Serve warm or at room temperature.

MAKES 4 TO 6 SERVINGS

HONEY CRUNCH GRANOLA

5 cups rolled oats
1 cup unsalted sunflower seeds
1/2 cup firmly packed light
brown sugar
2 teaspoons cinnamon
1 cup chopped pitted dates
1 cup raisins
10 tablespoons unsalted
butter, melted
1/2 cup honey
2 teaspoons vanilla extract

Combine the oats, sunflower kernels, brown sugar and cinnamon in a bowl. Add the dates and raisins and mix well. Mix the butter, honey and vanilla in a bowl. Pour over the oatmeal mixture. Toss for 1 minute. Spread on a greased rimmed baking sheet. Bake in a preheated 275-degree oven for $1^{1/4}$ hours or until crisp and golden brown, stirring occasionally. Cool completely. Store in an airtight container.

MAKES 9 CUPS

Each January, the free Cowboy Breakfast is the unofficial kick-off of the San Antonio Livestock Show and Rodeo. In 2001, it earned a Guinness World Record for serving 18,941 people in just one hour! Breakfast tacos, sausage biscuits, and live music offer a great way to start the day.

OVERNIGHT FRENCH TOAST

Cook the brown sugar and butter in a saucepan until melted. Add 2 tablespoons water, apples and cinnamon. Cook until the apples are slightly soft and the sauce is foamy. Pour the mixture into a greased 9×13-inch glass baking dish and cool. Cover with the Texas toast in a single layer or a double layer of white bread. Pour a mixture of the milk, eggs and vanilla evenly over the bread. Chill, covered, overnight. Bring almost to room temperature and bake in a preheated 350-degree oven for 40 minutes. Serve with syrup.

MAKES 6 SERVINGS

1 cup packed brown sugar
1/2 cup (1 stick) butter
  or margarine
3 green apples, peeled and
  thinly sliced
3/4 teaspoon cinnamon
6 slices Texas toast, or 12 slices
  white bread
1 1/2 cups milk
5 eggs
1 tablespoon vanilla extract

APRICOT FRENCH TOAST

Melt the butter in a saucepan and add the brown sugar and 2 teaspoons water. Cook until thick and foamy. Pour into a greased 9×13-inch baking dish. Cool for 10 minutes. Drain the apricots and spoon evenly into the baking dish. Sprinkle with almonds. Cover with a layer of bread. Pour a mixture of the eggs, milk and almond extract over the bread. Chill, covered, overnight. Bake, uncovered, in a preheated 350-degree oven for 30 to 40 minutes or until set. Sprinkle the top lightly with additional brown sugar. Bake for several minutes to brown. Cool for 5 to 10 minutes. Serve with whipped cream or yogurt.

MAKES 8 TO 10 SERVINGS

1/2 cup (1 stick) butter
1 cup packed brown sugar
Canned or fresh cooked apricots
Sliced almonds
French bread, sliced
6 eggs
1 1/2 cups milk
1 teaspoon almond extract

Pearl Bailey once stated that her kitchen was a place where odors from the past made a bridge to the future.

37

PAN MAÑANA

1/4 cup (1/2 stick) butter
1/3 cup granulated sugar
1/2 teaspoon cinnamon
1 teaspoon grated orange zest
2/3 cup orange juice
4 eggs, beaten
8 slices French bread
Confectioners' sugar

Melt the butter in a shallow 3-quart baking dish. Sprinkle with a mixture of the granulated sugar, cinnamon and orange zest. Combine the orange juice and eggs in a shallow bowl and mix well. Dip the bread slices into the egg mixture and arrange in a single layer over the butter mixture. Pour any remaining egg mixture over the bread. Chill, covered, overnight. Bake, uncovered, in a preheated 325-degree oven for 25 minutes. Sprinkle with confectioners' sugar.

MAKES 8 SERVINGS

TEXAS PECAN RING

1/2 cup (1 stick) margarine
(not butter)
1/4 cup maple syrup
3/4 cup packed light brown sugar
1 cup pecan pieces
2 (10-count) cans
refrigerator biscuits

Combine the margarine, syrup and brown sugar in a saucepan. Cook over low heat until the sugar dissolves and thickens slightly, stirring constantly. Stir in the pecans. Spray a bundt pan with nonstick cooking spray.

Pour three-fourths of the syrup mixture into the pan. Stand the biscuits on end around the inside of the pan. Pour the remaining syrup mixture over the biscuits. Bake in a preheated 350-degree oven for 25 minutes or until golden brown. Let stand for 3 minutes. Invert onto a large plate.

MAKES 10 SERVINGS

"All happiness depends on a leisurely breakfast."
—John Gunther

BLUEBERRY POPPY SEED BRUNCH CAKE

For the cake, beat the sugar and butter in a mixing bowl with an electric mixer until light and fluffy. Add the lemon zest and egg and beat at medium speed for 2 minutes. Spoon the flour lightly into a measuring cup and level off. Combine with the poppy seeds, baking soda and salt in a bowl. Add to the butter mixture alternately with the sour cream, beating after each addition until well blended. Spread the batter over the bottom and 1 inch up the side of a greased and floured 8- or 10-inch springform pan, making sure the batter on the sides is 3/4 inch thick.

For the filling and glaze, combine the blueberries, granulated sugar, flour and nutmeg in a bowl and mix well. Spoon over the batter. Bake in a preheated 350-degree oven for 45 to 55 minutes or until the cake is golden brown. Cool slightly. Remove the side of the pan.

Combine the confectioners' sugar with enough of the milk to make of glaze consistency in a small bowl. Drizzle over the warm cake.

MAKES 8 TO 10 SERVINGS

Cake

2/3 cup sugar

1/2 cup (1 stick) butter, softened

2 teaspoons grated lemon zest

1 egg

1 1/2 cups all-purpose flour

2 tablespoons poppy seeds

1/2 teaspoon baking soda

1/4 teaspoon salt

1/2 cup sour cream

Filling and Glaze

2 cups fresh or frozen blueberries, thawed, drained and patted dry

1/2 cup granulated sugar

2 teaspoons all-purpose flour

1/4 teaspoon nutmeg

1/2 cup confectioners sugar

1 to 2 teaspoons milk

FRESH APPLE OR PEACH MUFFINS

*1 cup chopped peeled apple
or peach
1 teaspoon lemon juice
1 cup milk
1 egg
1/4 cup vegetable oil
2/3 cup sugar
1/2 teaspoon salt
1/4 teaspoon cinnamon
1 tablespoon baking powder
2 cups unsifted all-purpose flour*

Sprinkle the apples with the lemon juice and set aside. Combine the milk, egg and oil in a bowl and mix well. Beat in the sugar, salt and cinnamon. Add the baking powder and flour and mix well. Fold in the apple mixture. Fill greased muffin cups two-thirds full. Bake in a preheated 450-degree oven for 20 minutes.

HIGHLAND MUFFINS

*3 eggs
2 cups sugar
1 cup canola oil
1 tablespoon vanilla extract
1 cup old-fashioned oats
(not instant)
2 cups whole wheat flour
2 1/2 teaspoons cinnamon
1/2 teaspoon ground allspice
1/2 teaspoon ground coriander
1 teaspoon baking soda
1 teaspoon salt
1/4 teaspoon baking powder
2 cups grated zucchini
1 cup chopped walnuts*

Beat the eggs and sugar in a bowl until well blended. Add the canola oil and vanilla and mix well. Stir in the oats, flour, cinnamon, allspice, coriander, baking soda, salt and baking powder. Stir in the zucchini and walnuts. Fill greased and floured muffin cups two-thirds full. Bake in a preheated 350-degree oven for 25 minutes.

Presented in a decorative container, muffins make a great gift. People of all ages can enjoy them for a meal or snack. To add a nice personal touch, include the recipe.

CHERRY SCONES

Combine the unbleached flour, whole wheat flour, granulated sugar, baking powder and salt in a bowl and mix well. Cut in the butter with your fingers or a pastry blender until the mixture resembles coarse meal. Stir in the cherries.

Combine the milk, egg and vanilla in a bowl. Pour over the dry mixture and stir just until mixed. Pat the dough into a 9-inch circle on a floured surface with lightly floured hands. Cut into 8 wedges. Sprinkle with the turbinado sugar. Arrange the wedges on a baking sheet. Bake in a preheated 350-degree oven for 20 to 25 minutes or until cooked through.

MAKES 8 SERVINGS

1 1/2 cups unbleached white flour

1/2 cup whole wheat flour

1/2 cup granulated sugar

2 teaspoons baking powder

1/2 teaspoon salt

1/4 cup (1/2 stick) unsalted
    butter, chilled

1 cup finely chopped
    dried cherries

1/2 cup nonfat milk

1 egg

1 1/2 teaspoons vanilla extract

1/4 cup turbinado sugar

ALL-IN-ONE BREAKFAST

Brown the sausage in a large ovenproof skillet, stirring until crumbly. Drain on paper towels. Return to the skillet. Spread the pie filling evenly over the sausage. Place the skillet in a hot oven to keep sizzling hot for a few minutes, but do not cook.

Pour the pancake batter evenly over the filling. Bake in a preheated 450-degree oven for 8 to 10 minutes or until light brown and a tester inserted in the center comes out clean. Cut into wedges. Serve immediately.

MAKES 6 TO 8 SERVINGS

16 ounces bulk pork sausage

1 (21-ounce) can apple pie filling

1 1/2 cups prepared pancake batter

41

MIGAS

1 green bell pepper,
cut into 1-inch pieces
1 small onion, chopped
1 serrano or jalapeño chile,
seeded and diced
1 garlic clove, minced
3 large plum tomatoes,
peeled and diced
1/4 cup fat-free chicken broth
1 teaspoon cumin
1/4 teaspoon salt
6 (5-inch) corn tortillas
3 eggs, beaten
4 egg whites, lightly beaten
1/4 teaspoon salt
1/2 cup (2 ounces) shredded
reduced-fat Cheddar cheese

Sauté the bell pepper, onion, serrano chile and garlic in a skillet sprayed with nonstick cooking spray for about 5 minutes. Add the tomatoes, broth, cumin and 1/4 teaspoon salt. Simmer, partially covered, for about 15 minutes. Remove from the skillet and keep warm.

Cut the tortillas into 1-inch strips, and then cut into halves crosswise. Cook the tortilla strips in a large skillet coated with cooking spray until crisp. Remove and keep warm. Add the eggs and egg whites to the skillet. Cook over medium heat without stirring until the eggs begin to set on the bottom. Draw a spatula across the bottom of the skillet to form large curds. Sprinkle with the tortilla strips and the remaining 1/4 teaspoon salt. Cook until the eggs are thickened but still moist. Spoon the vegetable mixture over the eggs. Sprinkle with the cheese and serve immediately.

MAKES 6 SERVINGS

The word "miga" or "migaja" is Spanish for "crumb." Made with tortilla crumbs, this breakfast dish originated in Texas. Although the meatless miga is a year-round favorite in San Antonio, this traditional dish gains popularity during Lent.

INDIVIDUAL SAUSAGE AND EGG PUFFS

Brown the sausage in a skillet, stirring until crumbly; drain. Brush nine 1-cup custard cups or ramekins with some of the melted butter and place on a baking sheet. Combine the remaining butter with the green chiles and mix well.

Beat the eggs in a large bowl. Stir in the Monterey Jack cheese, cottage cheese, flour, baking powder and salt. Add the chile mixture and sausage and mix well. Spoon the mixture evenly into the prepared cups.

Bake in a preheated 350-degree oven for 35 to 40 minutes or until a tester or knife inserted into the center comes out clean. Run a knife between the puff and the cup to loosen. Invert onto a plate and serve with fruit, sliced tomato or basil. Puffs can be wrapped in foil and frozen.

MAKES 9 SERVINGS

12 ounces bulk pork sausage

1/4 cup (1/2 stick) butter, melted

2 (4-ounce) cans chopped green chiles

12 eggs

1 pound shredded Monterey Jack cheese

2 cups cream-style cottage cheese

2/3 cup all-purpose flour

11/2 teaspoons baking powder

1/2 teaspoon salt

The April celebration known as Fiesta San Antonio began in 1891 with a simple parade to honor heroes from the Alamo and San Jacinto. Today, this ten-day city-wide party features three major parades, beauitfully dressed royalty, Night In Old San Antonio (NIOSA), festivals, carnivals, sporting events, and fireworks.

HAM AND BROCCOLI BRUNCH BAKE

2 cups cubed cooked ham
2 cups chopped fresh or thawed frozen broccoli
2 cups (8 ounces) shredded sharp Cheddar cheese
1 (6-ounce) package seasoned croutons
4 eggs, beaten
1 cup mayonnaise
2 tablespoons all-purpose flour
2 teaspoons dry mustard
2 teaspoons dried basil leaves

Combine the ham, broccoli, cheese and croutons in a bowl. Spread the mixture evenly in a 9×13-inch baking dish.

Combine the eggs, mayonnaise, flour, dry mustard and basil in a bowl and mix well. Pour over the ham mixture. Chill, covered, for 8 hours or longer. Bake, uncovered, in a preheated 375-degree oven for 1 hour. Slice and serve immediately.

MAKES 8 SERVINGS

GREEN CHILE EGG CASSEROLE

10 eggs
1/2 cup all-purpose flour
1 teaspoon baking powder
1/2 teaspoon salt
1 pound shredded Monterey Jack cheese
2 cups small curd cottage cheese
1/4 to 1/2 cup (1/2 to 1 stick) butter or margarine, melted
2 (4-ounce) cans chopped green chiles, drained

Beat the eggs in a bowl. Add the flour, baking powder, salt, Monterey Jack cheese, cottage cheese and butter and mix well. Stir in the green chiles. Pour into a buttered 9×13-inch baking dish. Bake in a preheated 350-degree oven for 35 to 45 minutes or until the top is brown and the center is firm.

MAKES 10 TO 12 SERVINGS

Southwestern and Asian recipes share a common dependence on chiles and cilantro. Cilantro is also known as "Chinese parsley." Coriander is the plant's seed.

BROOKE ARMY MEDICAL CENTER

Brooke Army Medical Center (BAMC) began as a small medical dispensary in 1897. Since its establishment, BAMC has been providing "responsive health care to U.S. service personnel, retirees, and their families."

JALAPEÑO QUICHE

1 pound bacon
1 pound shredded sharp
Cheddar cheese
8 eggs, beaten
1 onion, chopped
1/2 (12-ounce) jar pickled
jalapeños, diced
1/2 cup whole milk
Salt and pepper to taste

Fry the bacon in a skillet until crisp. Drain and crumble. Combine with the cheese, eggs, onion, jalapeño chiles, milk, salt and pepper in a bowl and mix well. Pour into a greased 7×11-inch baking dish. Bake in a preheated 350-degree oven for 45 minutes or until the top is brown. Cut into squares and serve. May add one-half medium bell pepper, chopped.

MAKES 6 SERVINGS

FIESTA TORTILLA QUICHES

12 medium flour tortillas
18 eggs
9 cups (36 ounces) grated
Monterey Jack cheese
1 (4-ounce) can chopped
green chiles
1/2 teaspoon seasoned salt
1/8 teaspoon pepper
1 cup evaporated milk
1/3 cup dried onion flakes
1/4 cup chopped red bell pepper
1/4 teaspoon garlic powder

Line twelve 4-inch pie plates with the tortillas. Combine the eggs, cheese, green chiles, salt, pepper, evaporated milk, onion flakes, bell pepper and garlic powder in a large bowl. Spoon about 3/4 cup of the mixture into each pie plate. Bake in a preheated 325-degree oven for 30 to 40 minutes or until a knife inserted in each center comes out clean. Serve with salsa, sour cream and chopped black olives. You may use Cheddar cheese, bacon and broccoli to vary the quiches.

MAKES 12 SERVINGS

The level of capsaicin in a chile determines its heat factor. Generally, the smaller the chile is in size, the hotter the flavor.

CRANBERRY SAUSAGE QUICHE

Let the pie shell stand at room temperature for 10 minutes. Do not prick the shell. Bake in a preheated 400-degree oven for 7 minutes. Set aside. Reduce the oven temperature to 375 degrees.

Cook the sausage and onion in a large skillet over medium-high heat, stirring until the sausage is brown and crumbly; drain. Remove from the heat and stir in the cranberries.

Sprinkle the cheese over the bottom of the pie shell. Top with the sausage mixture.

Whisk the eggs and half-and-half in a medium bowl until blended but not frothy. Pour over the sausage mixture. Bake for 40 to 45 minutes or until a knife inserted in the center comes out clean. Let stand for 10 minutes before serving. Garnish with fresh parsley or sage leaves. Store any leftovers in the refrigerator.

MAKES 6 SERVINGS

1 (9-inch) frozen deep-dish pie shell
8 ounces sage-flavored bulk pork sausage
1/4 cup chopped yellow onion
3/4 cup dried cranberries
1 1/2 cups (6 ounces) shredded Monterey Jack cheese
3 eggs, lightly beaten
1 1/2 cups half-and-half

Ever wondered how to recycle eggshells? In San Antonio, they're made into cascarónes. Puncture a hole in the egg's shell, blow out the egg's contents, and rinse out the shell. Then let the shell dry before painting the outside and filling the inside with confetti. Seal with a tissue paper patch. Breaking the cascarón over someone's head is supposed to bring them good luck.

SAUSAGE CASSEROLE

1 pound hot bulk pork sausage
1 pound Monterey Jack
cheese, shredded
1 cup milk
1 cup all-purpose flour
1 3/4 cups small curd
cottage cheese
6 eggs, beaten
1/4 cup (1/2 stick) butter, melted
1 (4-ounce) can chopped
green chiles

Brown the sausage in a skillet, stirring until brown and crumbly Spread over the bottom of a greased 9×13-inch glass baking dish. Combine the Monterey Jack cheese, milk, flour, cottage cheese, eggs, butter and green chiles in a large bowl and mix well. Pour the mixture over the sausage. Bake in a preheated 375-degree oven for 40 minutes or until set. Serve with picante sauce. The casserole can be assembled a day early. Store in the refrigerator and bake just before serving.

MAKES 12 SERVINGS

CHEESE PUDDING

10 slices bread, crusts
removed and bread cubed
1/2 cup (1 stick) butter
or margarine, melted
12 ounces shredded
Cheddar cheese
3 egg yolks
2 cups milk
1/2 teaspon red pepper
1/2 teaspoon salt
1/2 teaspoon dry mustard
3 egg whites

Arrange the bread in a greased 2-quart baking dish. Pour the melted butter over the the bread. Stir in the cheese.

Beat the egg yolks, milk, red pepper, salt and dry mustard in a bowl. Pour over the bread mixture. Beat the egg whites in a bowl until stiff peaks form. Fold into the bread mixture. Chill, covered, for 12 hours or longer. Bake in a preheated 350-degree oven for 45 minutes to 1 hour or until the top is brown and the center is set.

MAKES 6 TO 8 SERVINGS

CRESCENT SAUSAGE ROLL

Cook the sausage, onion and bell pepper in a large skillet, stirring until the sausage is brown and crumbly; drain. Stir the cream cheese and mushrooms into the hot mixture. Separate the crescent rolls into two rectangles. Shape the sausage mixture into two logs and arrange lengthwise down the center of each rectangle. Fold over the long side of the dough to enclose the filling. Place seam side down on an ungreased baking sheet. Brush with the egg whites and sprinkle with the poppy seeds. Bake in a preheated 350-degree oven for 20 minutes or until golden brown; cool. Cut into 1 1/2-inch slices to serve. The rolls may be frozen after baking.

MAKES 10 TO 12 SERVINGS

1 pound bulk pork sausage
1/2 cup chopped onion
1/2 cup chopped green bell pepper
8 ounces cream cheese
2 small cans sliced mushrooms
2 (8-count) packages crescent roll dough
2 egg whites, lightly beaten
1 to 2 tablespoons poppy seeds

SAUSAGE HASH BROWN BAKE

Brown the sausage in a large skillet over medium-high heat, stirring until crumbly; drain. Season the hash browns with 1/2 teaspoon salt and the pepper. Combine with the sausage and cheese in a bowl. Pour into a greased 9×13-inch baking dish. Beat the eggs, milk and 1 teaspoon salt in a bowl. Pour over the potato mixture. Bake in a preheated 350-degree oven for 35 to 40 minutes or until set. Serve hot.

MAKE 8 TO 10 SERVINGS

1 pound hot bulk pork sausage
1 pound mild bulk pork sausage
1 (30-ounce) package frozen hash brown potatoes, thawed
1/2 teaspoon salt
1/2 teaspoon pepper
2 cups (8 ounces) shredded Cheddar cheese
6 large eggs
2 cups milk
1 teaspoon salt

49

BRUNCH ENCHILADAS

1 pound cooked ham, cubed
1/2 cup chopped green onions
1 (4-ounce) can chopped
green chiles
1 pound shredded Monterey
Jack or Cheddar cheese
8 flour tortillas
10 eggs, beaten
1 1/4 cups half-and-half
1 tablespoon all-purpose flour
1/2 teaspoon salt

Mix the ham, green onions and green chiles in a bowl. Spoon about 2 tablespoons of the ham mixture and 2 tablespoons of the cheese onto each tortilla. Roll to enclose. Arrange seam side down in a greased 9×13-inch baking dish. Pour a mixture of the remaining ingredients evenly over the tortillas. Cover with plastic wrap and chill overnight. Bake in a preheated 350-degree oven for 45 minutes. Cover if tortillas begin to brown. Sprinkle with the remaining cheese. Bake until the cheese melts. Let stand for 10 minutes before serving.

MAKES 8 SERVINGS

BREAKFAST PIZZA

1/2 cup (1 stick) butter
or margarine
4 cups hash brown potatoes
1/2 cup chopped onion
1/2 cup chopped green bell pepper
6 eggs, well beaten
1 cup (4 ounces) shredded
Cheddar cheese
1/2 cup crumbled cooked bacon

Grease a pie plate with half the butter. Spread the hash brown potatoes over the bottom. Sauté the onion and bell pepper in the remaining 1/4 cup butter in a skillet. Combine with the eggs in a bowl and mix well. Pour over the hash browns. Sprinkle with the cheese and bacon. Bake in a preheated 350-degree oven for 30 minutes.

MAKES 6 SERVINGS

The debate over hash browns is about how they should be cut. Some prefer the potatoes to be finely shredded, while others want small chunks or thick strips. Most agree hash browns are best pan-fried and crispy.

50

HUEVOS RANCHEROS

Sauté the onion, bell pepper and garlic in the hot oil in a heavy skillet over low heat until the onion is translucent. Stir in the undrained tomatoes, green chiles, salt, pepper, chili powder, oregano and cumin. Simmer for 20 minutes. Make six wells in the sauce and carefully break one egg into each. Sprinkle with the cheese. Cook, covered, for 10 to 12 minutes. Serve with hot corn tortillas.

MAKES 6 SERVINGS

1 onion, chopped

1 green bell pepper, chopped

2 garlic cloves, crushed

1 tablespoon vegetable oil

1 (28-ounce) can peeled tomatoes, chopped

1 (4-ounce) can chopped green chiles

1 teaspoon salt

1/3 teaspoon pepper

1 teaspoon chili powder

1 teaspoon oregano

1/2 teaspoon ground cumin

6 eggs, at room temperature

1 1/2 cups (6 ounces) shredded Monterey Jack cheese

Proceeds from the San Antonio Stock Show and Rodeo are used to improve Texas agriculture and educate area youth. Along with livestock events, the rodeo offers world-class competition and entertainment for seventeen days each February.

SATISFYING
SOUPS, SALADS &
SANDWICHES

NOW SERVING:
INFORMATION THAT MAKES A DIFFERENCE

This cookbook is designed as a resource guide to benefit cooks of all experience levels. The **Watch Me Grow** booklet is designed to be a resource guide for parents of young children. The booklet pinpoints developmental, nutritional, and immunization information for caregivers of children, newborn through age five. Booklets are distributed to local school districts for their teen parenting programs, hospitals, and both public and private agencies (including agencies serviced through **Togs for Tots**). This publication can be found in both English and Spanish at www.alsanantonio.org.

In addition, the **Watch Me Grow** project finances the printing of "Breaking Away from Violence" cards. Distributed by the Battered Women's Shelter, the cards provide life-saving information for women who are being abused.

COME WATCH THE GAME!

Vegetable Squares page 21
Mexicorn Dip with Scoops page 26
Boot-Scootin' Chili page 127
Killer Corn Bread page 107
Kickoff Cherry-Chocolate Chunk Cookies page 162
Beer

PICNIC BY THE RIVER

Caponata page 18
Chilled Avocado Soup with Confetti Salsa page 54
Prosciutto, Fresh Mozzarella, Tomato and Basil Panini page 75
Italian Potato Salad page 68
Amaretto Chunk Cookies page 161
Iced Tea or Chianti

CREAM OF ARTICHOKE AND PECAN SOUP

4 onions, cut into quarters
3 tablespoons butter, melted
1/2 cup pecans, chopped
1/2 cup fresh basil, chopped
1/2 cup fresh parsley, chopped
Salt and pepper to taste
1/2 cup heavy cream
4 cups chicken broth
1/2 cup chopped artichoke hearts

Cook the onions in the butter in a medium saucepan over low heat for 15 to 25 minutes. Add the pecans and reduce the heat to medium. Cook for 10 to 15 minutes, stirring occasionally to prevent burning. Add the basil, parsley, salt and pepper. Cook for 5 minutes longer. Purée the mixture in a blender or food processor. Return to the saucepan and add the cream, broth and artichokes. Bring to a boil over low heat, then remove from heat immediately. Garnish with fresh basil.

MAKES 4 TO 6 SERVINGS

CHILLED AVOCADO SOUP WITH CONFETTI SALSA

4 avocadoes
2 tablespoons lime juice
1 large garlic clove, chopped
1/4 cup fresh cilantro leaves
1 tablespoon hot green pepper sauce
Salt to taste
3 cups water
2 red tomatoes, chopped
2 yellow tomatoes, chopped
1/2 small red onion, finely chopped
1 jalapeño chile, seeded and minced
1/4 cup fresh cilantro leaves, chopped
Pepper to taste

Process the avocadoes, lime juice, garlic, 1/4 cup cilantro, hot pepper sauce, salt and 2 cups of the water in a blender until smooth. Use the remaining 1 cup water to thin to the desired consistency. Cover tightly and chill. Combine the red tomatoes, yellow tomatoes, onion, jalapeño chile and 1/4 cup cilantro in a bowl and toss to combine. Season with salt and pepper. Ladle chilled soup into bowls or stemmed goblets. Top with the salsa.

MAKES 4 TO 6 SERVINGS

CREAM OF BRIE SOUP WITH TOASTY CROUTONS

Heat the broth with the bay leaf in a saucepan and set aside. Sauté the carrots, onion and celery in the butter in another saucepan. Sprinkle with the thyme and flour. Cook for 1 minute or until the flour is absorbed, stirring constantly. Discard the bay leaf and add the hot broth gradually, stirring constantly. Cook until thickened, stirring constantly.

Add the cheese and cook until melted, stirring constantly. Add the cream and heat through.

Cut leaf shapes from bread. Toast in a preheated 400-degree oven until crispy and brown. Ladle the soup into bowls and top with the croutons.

MAKES 6 SERVINGS

$3^1/2$ cups high-quality vegetable broth
1 bay leaf
1 cup minced carrots
1 cup minced onion
1 cup minced celery
6 tablespoons butter, melted
1 teaspoon thyme
$1/3$ cup all-purpose flour
6 to 8 ounces Brie cheese, rind removed and cheese cut into chunks
$1/2$ cup heavy cream
White bread slices

CHILLED FRUIT SOUP

Combine the fruit, yogurt, milk, sugar and cinnamon in a blender. Cover and process until smooth. Refrigerate until chilled. Ladle into bowls and serve as an appetizer or soup course. Garnish with fruit before serving.

MAKES 4 SERVINGS

3 cups sliced fruit (all one type)
1 cup vanilla yogurt
$1/2$ cup lowfat milk
1 tablespoon sugar
$1/4$ teaspoon cinnamon

"Chilled soup is summer comfort at its best."
—Mark Vogel

55

CRAB AND CORN CHOWDER

1/2 cup chopped green onions
1 garlic clove, minced
1/2 teaspoon cayenne pepper
2 tablespoons butter
2 (10-ounce) cans cream of potato soup
8 ounces reduced-fat cream cheese, softened
1 cup 1% milk
1 cup nonfat cream
1 (6-ounce) can crab meat
1 (16-ounce) can whole kernel corn
1 tablespoon sugar

Sauté the onions, garlic, and cayenne pepper in the butter in a saucepan until tender. Stir in the soup, cream cheese, milk and cream. Cook over medium-low heat until well blended, stirring occasionally. Drain and flake the crab meat. Stir the undrained corn and crab meat into the soup. Reduce the heat to simmer and cook for 10 minutes. Stir in the sugar.

If you prefer, you may substitute two shredded cooked chicken breasts for the crab meat.

MAKES 6 SERVINGS

CREAM OF PECAN SOUP WITH CHIPOTLE CREAM

1/2 onion, finely chopped
1/2 cup finely chopped celery
2 tablespoons butter, melted
3 garlic cloves, crushed
2 tablespoons tomato paste
8 ounces pecans, toasted
8 cups chicken broth
1 whole chipotle chile in adobo sauce
2 tablespoons maple syrup
Dash of Worcestershire sauce
Salt and pepper to taste
1 cup heavy cream

Sauté the onion and celery in the butter in a heavy saucepan until tender. Add the garlic and sauté for 1 minute. Stir in the tomato paste. Combine the pecans, 1 cup of the broth and the chipotle chile in a blender and process until well combined. Add to the saucepan along with the remaining 7 cups broth. Bring to a simmer, stirring frequently. Add the maple syrup, Worcestershire sauce, salt and pepper. Cook for 5 minutes. Reduce the heat and stir in the cream. Ladle into bowls and garnish with crème fraîche, chopped chives, pecan halves or thin strips of chipotle chile.

MAKES 8 SERVINGS

CHEESY POTATO SOUP

Peel and cube the potatoes. Combine with the onion, carrots, celery, broth, 1 soup can water, salt and pepper in a large saucepan. Bring to a boil and cook for 15 to 30 minutes or until the vegetables are tender. Mash the vegetables to desired texture. Add the cheese and milk and cook until heated through.

MAKES 6 SERVINGS

2 or 3 large baking potatoes

1/2 onion, chopped

1/2 cup chopped carrots

1/2 cup chopped celery

1 (14-ounce) can chicken broth

1 teaspoon salt

1/2 teaspoon pepper

1 cup cubed reduced-fat Velveeta

1 cup skim milk

BAKED POTATO SOUP

Bake the potatoes until very tender. Cool and peel. Cut into cubes.

Melt the butter in a saucepan. Stir in the flour and cook until smooth, stirring constantly. Add the milk gradually and cook until thickened, stirring constantly. Add the potatoes and green onions. Bring to a boil, stirring constantly. Reduce the heat to low and simmer for 10 minutes. Add the bacon, cheese, sour cream, salt and pepper and cook until the cheese is melted, stirring constantly. Garnish with additional cheese, bacon and green onions.

MAKES 8 TO 10 SERVINGS

4 large russet potatoes

2/3 cup butter

2/3 cup all-purpose flour

7 cups whole milk

4 green onions, sliced

12 strips bacon, crisp-cooked
    and crumbled

1 1/4 cups (5 ounces) shredded
    sharp Cheddar cheese

1 cup sour cream

3/4 teaspoon salt

1/2 teaspoon pepper

POSOLE

1¹/2 pounds pork, cubed
2 onions, chopped
2 tablespoons vegetable oil
¹/2 cup chile powder, or to taste
1 tablespoon all-purpose flour
1 teaspoon salt
¹/2 teaspoon oregano
1 garlic clove, chopped
4 cups hot water
1 (15-ounce) can hominy

Brown the pork and onions in the oil in a large saucepan until the onions are translucent. Add the chile powder and flour and mix well. Stir in the salt, oregano, garlic and water. Cook, covered, over low heat for 2¹/2 hours or until the pork is tender. Skim the fat as needed and add water if the mixture seems too thick or is sticking to the saucepan.

Add the hominy and cook, covered, for 30 minutes longer. Serve in soup bowls and garnish with green onions and cubed cream cheese. Offer lime wedges or top posole with a drizzle of lime juice.

MAKES 4 TO 6 SERVINGS

PUMPKIN SOUP

1 cup finely chopped celery
¹/2 cup chopped onion
1 cup chopped carrots
2 tablespoons butter
2 cups canned pumpkin
4 cups homemade chicken broth
1 teaspoon salt
¹/4 teaspoon pepper
¹/4 teaspoon thyme
¹/8 teaspoon ground ginger

Sauté the celery, onion and carrots in the butter in a large saucepan for 5 minutes. Add the pumpkin and mix well. Add the broth, salt, pepper and thyme. Simmer for 1 hour; cool. Purée in a blender. Return to the saucepan. Reheat and add the ginger. Ladle into bowls and garnish with sour cream. This soup is best if made a day ahead and chilled. Reheat the soup without boiling, adding the ginger just before serving.

MAKES 8 TO 10 SERVINGS

GAZPACHO

Combine the tomato purée, onion, bell pepper and cucumber in a blender. Process at high speed for 30 seconds. Pour into a serving bowl. Combine the tomato juice, olive oil, vinegar, garlic, salt and cumin in a bowl and mix well. Add to the tomato mixture. Chill for 2 hours or longer. Serve with croutons and garnish with chopped bell peppers and cucumbers.

MAKES 8 SERVINGS

2 cups canned tomato purée
1 small onion, chopped
1 green bell pepper, chopped
1 small cucumber, chopped
2 cups tomato juice
1/4 cup olive oil
3 tablespoons white vinegar
1 small garlic clove, minced
1 teaspoon salt
1/4 teaspoon cumin

"DOWN UNDER"
TOMATO BASIL SOUP

Combine the ham hock, carrot and onion with water to cover in a saucepan. Bring to a boil. Reduce the heat and simmer for 30 minutes. Strain, reserving the broth. Remove the ham from the bone and chop finely. Melt 2 tablespoons butter in a medium saucepan. Add the tomatoes and cook until soft. Add 1/4 cup butter and the flour and cook for 2 minutes. Remove from the heat and add the tomato paste and basil. Add the reserved broth and chopped ham and bring to a boil. Simmer for 30 to 45 minutes. Process in batches in a food processor until blended. Return to the saucepan. Dissolve the brown sugar in the vinegar in a bowl and add to the soup. Season to taste and serve.

MAKES 6 TO 8 SERVINGS

1 ham hock
1 large carrot, coarsely chopped
1 large onion, coarsely chopped
2 tablespoons butter
31/2 pounds ripe tomatoes, peeled
   and coarsely chopped
1/4 cup (1/2 stick) butter
3/4 cup plus 2 tablespoons
   all-purpose flour
1 (6-ounce) can tomato paste
3 tablespoons dried basil
   or oregano
3 tablespoons brown sugar
2 generous tablespoons
   malt vinegar

59

TACO SOUP

2 pounds ground beef or
ground turkey
1 large onion, finely chopped
1 (15-ounce) can pinto beans
with jalapeño chiles
1 (16-ounce) can kidney beans
1 (14-ounce) can stewed
tomatoes
1 (11-ounce) can shoepeg corn
1 (4-ounce) can chopped mild
green chiles, optional
1 envelope taco seasoning mix
1 envelope ranch dressing mix
2¹/4 cups water

Brown the ground beef with the onion in a skillet, stirring until the beef is crumbly; drain. Add the undrained beans, tomatoes, corn and green chiles and mix well. Stir in the taco seasoning mix and ranch dressing mix. Add the water and mix well. Simmer for 30 minutes or longer. Serve with tortilla chips.

MAKES 6 SERVINGS

Mission San Francisco de la Espada was founded by the Franciscan missionaries who sought to build a community similar to a Spanish village. In this community, Native Americans were taught the skills of weaving and the use of farm and carpentry tools.

APPLE SPINACH SALAD

Combine the sugar, canola oil, vinegar and celery salt in a bowl or a jar with a tight-fitting lid. Whisk or shake to blend.

Peel and chop the apples. Toss the spinach, apples and raisins in a bowl. Top with the dressing. Add the cashews just before serving. You may substitute glazed walnuts or glazed pecans for the cashews.

MAKES 6 TO 9 SERVINGS

1/4 cup sugar

1/4 cup canola oil

2 tablespoons balsamic or apple cider vinegar

1/4 teaspoon celery salt

2 Granny Smith apples

2 (10-ounce) packages fresh baby spinach

1/4 cup golden raisins

1/2 cup salted cashews

ORANGE AND CANDIED ALMOND SALAD

Combine the oil, vinegar, 2 tablespoons sugar, Tabasco sauce, salt and pepper in a bowl or a jar with a tight-fitting lid. Whisk or shake to blend.

Combine the almonds and 3 tablespoons sugar in a heavy-bottomed saucepan. Heat until the sugar melts, stirring to coat the almonds. Pour onto waxed paper or foil and let cool. Break apart and store in an airtight container. Combine the iceberg lettuce, romaine, celery and green onions in a salad bowl and toss. Top with the almonds, oranges and dressing and serve.

MAKES 4 TO 6 SERVINGS

1/4 cup vegetable oil

2 tablespoons vinegar

2 tablespoons sugar

Tabasco sauce to taste

1/2 teaspoon salt

1/8 teaspoon pepper

1/2 cup sliced almonds

3 tablespoons sugar

1/2 head iceberg lettuce

1/2 head romaine

1 cup chopped celery

2 green onions, chopped

1 (11-ounce) can mandarin oranges

ARTICHOKE RICE SALAD

1 (8-ounce) package chicken-
flavored vermicelli rice mix
1 (6-ounce) package fried rice
mix with almonds
1/2 cup chopped green bell pepper
1/2 cup chopped green onions
1/2 cup chopped
pimento-stuffed olives
2 (6-ounce) jars marinated
artichoke hearts,
drained and sliced
1/2 cup mayonnaise
1 teaspoon curry powder

Prepare the vermicelli rice mix and fried rice mix according to the package directions; cool.

Combine the rice in a large bowl. Add the bell pepper, green onions, olives, artichoke hearts, mayonnaise and curry powder. Toss lightly to coat. Chill until serving time.

MAKES 12 SERVINGS

An artichoke is actually a flowering thistle that originated in the Mediterranean—perhaps North Africa or Sicily—and was brought to Florence, Italy, by the middle of the fifteenth century.

SPINACH BLUES SALAD WITH BLUEBERRY DRESSING

Combine the shallot, 1/2 pint blueberries, salt, sugar, vinegar and oil in a blender. Process until well blended. Chill until serving time. Toss the spinach, 1 pint blueberries, cheese and pecans in a large bowl. Add the dressing, tossing to coat.

MAKES 4 TO 6 SERVINGS

1 shallot, minced

1/2 pint fresh blueberries

1 tablespoon salt

3 tablespoons sugar

1/3 cup raspberry vinegar

1 cup vegetable oil

10 ounces fresh spinach

1 pint fresh blueberries

2/3 cup crumbled blue cheese

1/2 cup toasted pecans, chopped

BROCCOLI SALAD

Combine the mayonnaise, sour cream, vinegar and sugar in a bowl and mix well. Combine the broccoli, grapes, onions and celery in a bowl and mix well. Add the dressing and toss to coat. Chill for 8 hours or longer. Add the walnuts and bacon just before serving.

MAKES 6 SERVINGS

Each type of vinegar has a distinctive flavor. The well-rounded flavor of red wine vinegar is a favorite of many cooks. White wine vinegar should be used with light-colored foods. Cider vinegar has a fruitier taste, while malt vinegar's taste is stronger.

1/2 cup mayonnaise

1/2 cup sour cream

2 tablespoons wine vinegar

1 tablespoon sugar

6 cups frozen broccoli, cooked
    and well drained

3/4 cup each red seedless grapes
    and white seedless grapes,
    cut into halves

2 green onions, chopped

1 cup chopped celery

2/3 cup walnut pieces

6 slices bacon, crisp-cooked
    and crumbled

63

CRUNCHY RAMEN SLAW

1/3 cup olive oil
1/3 cup red wine vinegar
1/3 cup sugar
2 packages chicken-flavored ramen noodles
1 (16-ounce) package coleslaw mix
1 cup sunflower seeds
1 cup slivered almonds
1 bunch green onions, chopped

Combine the olive oil, vinegar, sugar and flavor packets from the ramen noodles in a bowl or a jar with a tight-fitting lid. Whisk or shake to blend.

Combine the coleslaw mix, sunflower seeds, almonds and green onions in a bowl and toss.

Crush the ramen noodles and add to the coleslaw mixture. Add the dressing, tossing to coat.

MAKES 10 SERVINGS

SPICY THAI CHICKEN SALAD

1 pound cooked chicken, cut into 1/2-inch pieces
3 cups cooked white rice
6 cups coleslaw mix
1/4 cup chopped cilantro
3 carrots, julienned
6 green onions, chopped
1 (11-ounce) bottle Thai peanut sauce
1/4 cup vegetable oil
1/4 cup water
3/4 cup coarsely chopped dry-roasted peanuts

Combine the chicken, rice, coleslaw mix, cilantro, carrots and green onions in a bowl and mix well. Whisk the peanut sauce, oil and water in a bowl. Add to the rice mixture and toss to coat. Top with the peanuts to serve.

MAKES 6 SERVINGS

"All you need to become a good cook is curiosity and a sense of adventure."
—Anne Willan

MANDARIN CHICKEN SALAD

For the dressing, combine the water, soy sauce, vinegar, sherry, sugar, garlic and ginger in a bowl or jar with a tight-fitting lid. Whisk or shake to blend. Add the peanut butter and whisk or shake to blend.

For the salad, arrange the romaine in a 9- or 10-inch glass bowl. Drizzle 2 to 3 tablespoons of the dressing over the romaine. Arrange the noodles over the romaine. Spoon the sesame oil over the noodles. Drizzle 2 to 3 tablespoons of the dressing over the noodles. Arrange the chicken strips over the noodles. Pour the remaining dressing over the chicken strips. Sprinkle the green onions and peanuts over the salad. Arrange the oranges over the salad. Serve immediately.

MAKES 4 OR 5 SERVINGS

Peanut Soy Dressing

6 tablespoons water

1/4 cup soy sauce

4 teaspoons red wine vinegar

3 tablespoons cream sherry

2 teaspoons sugar

1 1/2 garlic cloves, minced

2 tablespoons chopped peeled
    fresh ginger

1/4 cup creamy peanut butter

Salad

8 to 10 leaves romaine, shredded

3 ounces rice chow mein noodles

6 tablespoons sesame oil

2 chicken breasts, cooked and
    cut into strips

4 or 5 green onions, thinly sliced

1/2 cup chopped dry-roasted
    peanuts

2 oranges, sectioned or sliced

Though peanut butter is often the ingredient for children's sandwiches, it can provide an appealing taste in adult recipes.

65

HEARTS OF PALM SALAD WITH BASIL GARLIC DRESSING

Basil Garlic Dressing

1/2 cup white wine vinegar
1/4 cup lemon juice
8 fresh basil leaves
3 garlic cloves
1/4 teaspoon salt
1/4 teaspoon pepper
3/4 cup olive oil

Salad

2 (14-ounce) cans hearts of palm, drained and cut into 1/2-inch slices
2 red or yellow bell peppers, cut into strips
1 pint cherry tomatoes
1 red onion, thinly sliced and separated into rings
5 to 6 heads Bibb lettuce

For the dressing, combine the vinegar, lemon juice, basil, garlic, salt and pepper in a blender. Process on high, leaving the motor running. Add the olive oil gradually in a slow, steady stream, processing for 2 minutes. Chill, covered, overnight. Process again before serving.

For the salad, combine the hearts of palm, bell peppers, tomatoes and onion in a large bowl. Arrange the lettuce in a salad bowl or on individual plates. Top with the vegetable mixture and drizzle with the dressing.

MAKES 12 SERVINGS

In 1905, Florence Butt started the C.C. Butt Grocery Store in Kerrville, Texas. When her son, Howard E., took over in 1919, he adopted the motto, "He profits most who serves best." In 1985, the HEB grocery chain moved its corporate headquarters to San Antonio.

MANGO SOUFFLE SALAD

Soften the gelatin in the cold water in a small bowl. Combine the reserved mango juice with enough water to measure 2 cups in a saucepan and bring to a boil. Pour over the gelatin, stirring to dissolve the gelatin. Let cool. Purée the mangoes in a blender. Add the cream cheese cubes gradually, blending until smooth. Stir into the gelatin mixture. Pour into an oiled 2-quart mold. Chill until set. Unmold to serve.

MAKES 8 SERVINGS

2 (3-ounce) packages lemon gelatin
1/2 cup cold water
1 (27-ounce) can mangoes, juice drained and reserved
1 envelope unflavored gelatin
8 ounces cream cheese, cubed

JICAMA SLAW

Combine the lime juice, vinegar and olive oil in a bowl or a jar with a tight-fitting lid. Whisk or shake to blend. Season with salt and pepper.

Combine the jicama, bell peppers, jalapeño chile, onion, cilantro, cabbage and carrots in a large bowl and mix well. Add the dressing and toss to coat.

MAKES 12 SERVINGS

Jicama, a tuber with a sweet, nutty flavor and juicy crispness, can be eaten raw or cooked. Need a new snack food? Try jicama instead of a carrot.

Juice of 2 limes (about 1/4 cup)
2 tablespoons vinegar
3 tablespoons olive oil or canola oil
Salt and pepper to taste
1 small jicama, peeled and julienned
1 small yellow bell pepper, sliced
1 small green bell pepper, sliced
1 small red bell pepper, sliced
1 large jalapeño chile, seeded and sliced
1/2 small red onion, sliced
1/4 cup cilantro, chopped
1 small head red cabbage, cut into halves and sliced
1 cup shredded carrots

ITALIAN POTATO SALAD

1/4 cup light olive oil

6 tablespoons white wine vinegar

1 tablespoon oregano

Salt and pepper to taste

6 red potatoes,
cut into cubes and cooked

1 (12-ounce) can Italian
green beans

1/3 cup thinly sliced green onions

2 cups cherry or grape tomatoes,
cut into halves

1 cup artichoke hearts,
drained and chopped

4 ounces feta cheese, crumbled

1/3 cup grated Parmesan cheese

1 (2-ounce) can black
olives, sliced

Combine the olive oil, vinegar, oregano, salt and pepper in a bowl or a jar with a tight-fitting lid. Whisk or shake to blend.

Toss the potatoes, green beans, green onions, tomatoes, artichoke hearts, feta cheese, Parmesan cheese and olives in a large bowl. Add the dressing and toss to coat. The salad may be prepared a day in advance and refrigerated.

MAKES 8 TO 10 SERVINGS

The State motto of Texas is "Friendship." Assistance League of San Antonio serves as an example of this guiding principle by extending friendship to the local community through its Thrift House and philanthropic projects.

68

SPECHT'S STORE

Established in 1890 as a general store, Specht's now serves three meals a day,
Wednesday through Sunday. When looking for a place to kick back and
enjoy fried catfish and onion rings while listening to the lively
lyrics of newly emerging singing cowboys or nostalgic tunes from the past,
Specht's just might be the place to go.

ORIENTAL SHRIMP SALAD

Creamy Soy Dressing
3/4 cup mayonnaise
2 tablespoons soy sauce
1 tablespoon lemon juice
3/8 teaspoon ground ginger
1/4 teaspoon MSG (optional)

Salad
8 ounces shrimp, boiled and peeled
1 (14-ounce) can bean sprouts
*1 (8-ounce) can water
chestnuts, chopped*
1/4 cup chopped celery
1/4 cup chopped onion
*1 (6-ounce) can
chow mein noodles*

For the dressing, combine the mayonnaise, soy sauce, lemon juice, ginger and MSG in a bowl or a jar with a tight-fitting lid. Whisk or shake to blend.

For the salad, cut each shrimp into two or three pieces. Combine with the bean sprouts, water chestnuts, celery and onion in a salad bowl. Combine the salad, dressing and chow mein noodles and mix well.

MAKES 8 SERVINGS

SPINACH AND BASIL SALAD

6 cups fresh spinach leaves
2 cups fresh basil leaves
1/2 cup olive oil
3 garlic cloves, minced
1/2 cup pine nuts
*4 ounces prosciutto, thinly sliced
and finely chopped*
Salt and pepper to taste
*1/2 cup (2 ounces) grated
Parmesan cheese*

Combine the spinach and basil in a large bowl. Heat the olive oil in a medium skillet over medium heat. Add the garlic and pine nuts and sauté until the pine nuts begin to brown slightly. Stir in the prosciutto and cook for 1 minute longer. Season with salt and pepper. Pour the mixture over the spinach mixture and toss to coat. Sprinkle with the cheese. Serve with freshly ground pepper and additional Parmesan cheese.

MAKES 4 TO 6 SERVINGS

70

STROGANOFF STEAK SANDWICHES

Combine the beer, oil, salt, garlic powder and pepper in a shallow dish and mix well. Add the steak and turn to coat. Marinate, covered, in the refrigerator overnight. Drain the steak, discarding the marinade. Broil 3 inches from the heat source for 6 minutes on each side for medium rare or to the desired degree of doneness. Slice across the grain into thin slices.

Melt the butter with the paprika and salt in a skillet. Add the onions and cook until tender. Arrange the onions on the bread. Top with the sliced steak. Combine the sour cream and horseradish in a saucepan and heat until warm. Spoon some of the mixture over the steak. Sprinkle with paprika to taste.

MAKES 6 SERVINGS

2/3 cup beer

1/3 cup vegetable oil

1 to 2 teaspoons salt

1/4 to 1/2 teaspoon garlic powder

1/4 to 1/2 teaspoon pepper

2 pounds flank steak,
    cut 1-inch thick

2 tablespoons butter, melted

1/2 teaspoon paprika, or to taste

Salt to taste

2 cups sliced onions

6 slices French bread,
    toasted and buttered

1 cup sour cream

1/2 to 1 teaspoon prepared
    horseradish

Paprika to taste

Founded in 1851, Ursuline Academy, a French preparatory school for girls, was built on the San Antonio River. Ursuline remained an educational institution until 1965. Today, it houses instructional studios and exhibit space for individuals interested in creating and experiencing art.

STROMBOLI SANDWICH

1¹/2 pounds ground round
1 small onion, chopped
1 small green bell pepper, chopped
¹/3 cup sliced mushrooms
1 (12-ounce) can tomato paste
¹/4 cup water
¹/4 cup (1 ounce) grated
Parmesan cheese
¹/2 teaspoon dried oregano
¹/2 teaspoon garlic powder
¹/4 teaspoon crushed rosemary
¹/4 teaspoon dried sage
Salt and pepper to taste
4 (8-ounce) loaves French bread
16 ounces mozzarella cheese,
shredded or sliced

Brown the ground beef in a skillet, stirring until crumbly; drain. Add the onion, bell pepper and mushrooms. Cook for 5 minutes. Stir in the tomato paste, water, Parmesan cheese, oregano, garlic powder, rosemary, sage, salt and pepper. Simmer for 20 minutes, stirring occasionally. Adjust the seasonings to taste. Cut the top one-third from each loaf of bread lengthwise. Scoop out the centers. (Leftover bread may be used for bread crumbs.) Line the shells with some of the mozzarella cheese. Fill with ground beef mixture. Cover with the remaining mozzarella cheese. Replace the tops of the bread. Bake, wrapped securely in foil, in a preheated 400-degree oven for 6 to 10 minutes. Cut into 2-inch slices with a serrated knife.

MAKES 12 SERVINGS

ROAST BEEF SANDWICH WITH HORSERADISH CREAM

2 ounces light cream
cheese, softened
1 teaspoon prepared
horseradish, drained
¹/2 teaspoon Dijon mustard
12 slices pumpernickel bread
12 gherkin sweet pickles, minced
24 very thin slices roast beef
Salt and pepper to taste

Mix the cream cheese, horseradish and Dijon mustard in a small bowl. Lightly toast the bread. Spread 1 teaspoon of the cream cheese mixture on one side of six bread slices. Sprinkle evenly with the pickles. Top with four slices of roast beef. Season with salt and pepper. Top with the remaining bread slices. Cut diagonally, or leave open-face and cut into quarters for a lighter sandwich.

MAKES 6 SERVINGS

72

TORTA RUSTICA

Combine the flour, cornmeal and salt in a medium bowl. Cut in the butter with a pastry blender until the mixture resembles coarse crumbs. Beat 2 eggs with the water. Stir into the flour mixture until a dough forms. Add 1 tablespoon water if dough seems dry. Shape two-thirds of the dough into a disk and wrap tightly in plastic wrap. Repeat with the remaining dough. Chill for 30 minutes or until firm enough to roll. Mix the cottage cheese, feta cheese, Parmesan cheese, 1 egg, parsley, basil and oregano in a bowl.

Roll out the larger portion of dough to fit an 8- or 9-inch springform pan within 1 inch of the top rim. Reroll scraps to cut into decorative shapes for the top, if desired. Scatter 1 cup mozzarella cheese over the bottom. Arrange half the ham slices on top in an even layer. Spread with the cottage cheese mixture and cover with the spinach. Cover with the remaining ham slices. Press down gently to compact the layers. Add the red peppers in a single layer and top with 1 cup mozzarella cheese. Roll out the remaining dough to an 8- or 9-inch circle. Place over the filling. Moisten the edge of the top crust and press lightly to seal. Crimp or flute the edge.

Brush the top with 1 beaten egg. Cut several steam vents in the top. Bake in a preheated 375-degree oven for 1 hour or until the crust is deep golden brown and pulls away from the side of the pan. Cool in the pan on a wire rack for 45 minutes. Remove the side of the pan; cool. Cut into 12 wedges. Serve at room temperature.

MAKES 12 SERVINGS

2 1/4 cups all-purpose flour

3/4 cup yellow cornmeal

1/2 teaspoon salt

3/4 cup (1 1/2 sticks) butter, chilled and cut into small pieces

2 eggs

3 tablespoons cold water

1 1/2 cups small curd cottage cheese

4 ounces feta cheese, crumbled

1 cup (4 ounces) grated Parmesan cheese

1 egg

1/4 cup chopped fresh parsley

2 tablespoons finely chopped fresh basil, or 2 teaspoons dried basil

2 teaspoons finely chopped fresh oregano, or 1 teaspoon dried oregano

1 cup (4 ounces) shredded mozzarella cheese

8 ounces Black Forest ham, thinly sliced and patted dry

1 (10-ounce) package frozen chopped spinach, thawed and squeezed dry

1 (7-ounce) jar roasted red peppers, rinsed, drained and patted dry

1 cup (4 ounces) shredded mozzarella cheese

1 egg, slightly beaten

73

FAMILY-STYLE MUFFULETTA

1 cup packed fresh basil leaves
1/2 cup olive oil
1/2 cup pitted kalamata olives
1/4 cup capers, drained
1 tablespoon chopped garlic
Salt and pepper to taste
1 (2-pound) round loaf
sourdough bread
12 ounces salami, thinly sliced
12 ounces provolone cheese,
thinly sliced
2 (7-ounce) jars roasted
red peppers, drained
1 large red or white onion,
thinly sliced
6 plum tomatoes, sliced

Process the basil, olive oil, olives, capers and garlic in a food processor until the basil and olives are finely chopped. Season with salt and pepper. May be made a day ahead and chilled, covered.

Cut the bread into halves horizontally. Pull or cut out enough of the bread to leave a 1 1/2-inch-thick shell. Spread half the basil dressing inside the bottom bread shell. Layer with half the salami, cheese, peppers, onion and tomatoes. Repeat to form the second layer. Spread the remaining dressing on the cut side of the top bread half. Press over the filling. Chill, wrapped tightly with plastic wrap, for 1 hour or longer. Cut into wedges to serve. May be prepared a day ahead and refrigerated.

MAKES 6 SERVINGS

The muffuletta, which originated in New Orleans, is prepared with layers of green and black olives, roasted bell peppers, sun-dried tomatoes, salami, ham, and provolone cheese. A muffuletta can be served as a hearty appetizer or as an entrée sandwich.

PROSCIUTTO, FRESH MOZZARELLA, TOMATO AND BASIL PANINI

Whisk the olive oil, vinegar and garlic in a small bowl to blend. Season with salt and pepper.

Layer the prosciutto, cheese, tomatoes and basil over the bottom half of the ciabatta. Drizzle lightly with the dressing and sprinkle with salt and pepper. Replace the remaining ciabatta half on top and press down. Cut into four servings.

Heat a panini grill, flat-top grill or a heavy skillet. Grill the sandwiches for about 5 minutes per side or until the bread is golden brown and the cheese melts, pressing occasionally with a spatula. You can also press the sandwiches with a baking sheet.

MAKES 4 SERVINGS

1/2 cup extra-virgin olive oil

3 tablespoons balsamic vinegar

1 large garlic clove, minced

Kosher or sea salt to taste

Freshly ground pepper to taste

8 ounces prosciutto, thinly sliced

10 ounces fresh mozzarella cheese, thinly sliced

12 tomato slices

12 large fresh basil leaves

1 (1-pound) ciabatta, cut into halves horizontally, or small panini-style crusty rolls

Prosciutto is a delicately flavored Italian ham made from the meat of a hog's hindquarters. Prosciutto crudo is cured and served in appetizers. Prosciutto cotto is boiled and used in sandwiches and main dishes.

75

*A shady corner in the gardens of the Antique Rose Emporium
makes a scenic setting for a delicious lunch with friends.*

LUSCIOUS LUNCHEONS & TEAS

NOW SERVING:
THE GIFT OF FRIENDSHIP

People are the perfect accompaniment to the luscious foods served at luncheons and teas. Sharing food with family and friends gives us a sense of well-being and belonging.

Some assisted-living residents have lost this sense of belonging. They no longer have relationships that make them feel special. The **Adopt A Resident** project offers nursing home residents the gift of friendship through one-on-one relationships with Assistance League® members.

In addition, the volunteers also assist with special events and field trips, help with monthly birthday parties, lead a preset exercise program, give mini manicures to residents, and make centerpieces for holiday dinners. Volunteers indicate that they receive as much joy as they try to provide.

LUNCHEON FOR THE LADIES

Shrimp or Lobster Bisque with Oyster Crackers page 83
Hot Herbed Chicken Sandwich page 79
Basil and Tomato Salad page 84
Cherry Scones page 41
Lemon Chess Pie page 146
Hot or Iced Ginger Tea
Chablis

MINIATURE BEEF WELLINGTONS

Beef Wellingtons

3 tablespoons butter

8 (3-ounce) beef tenderloin
fillets, 1 inch thick

1/4 teaspoon salt

1/4 teaspoon pepper

2 tablespoons butter

3 large fresh mushrooms,
chopped

1 (8-ounce) package fresh
mushrooms, chopped

2 tablespoons dry sherry or
beef broth

1 (17-ounce) package frozen puff
pastry sheets, thawed

1 egg white, lightly beaten

Espagnole Sauce

1 1/2 tablespoons butter

1 1/2 tablespoons all-purpose flour

1 tablespoon tomato paste

2 (14-ounce) cans beef broth

1 bay leaf

For the beef Wellingtons, melt 3 tablespoons butter in a large skillet over medium heat. Add the fillets and cook for 3 minutes on each side or until brown. Remove from the skillet and season with the salt and pepper. Set aside to cool.

Melt 2 tablespoons butter in the skillet. Add the mushrooms and sauté for 5 minutes. Stir in the sherry. Unfold one pastry sheet on a lightly floured surface. Roll to 1/8-inch thickness. Cut into fourths. Place a fillet in the center of each pastry square. Top with the mushroom mixture. Bring opposite corners of the squares together over the beef, pressing gently to seal. Repeat with the remaining pastry sheet and fillets.

Arrange the beef Wellingtons on a baking sheet and brush with the egg white. Bake on the lowest oven rack in a preheated 425-degree oven for 25 to 30 minutes or until the pastry is golden brown.

For the sauce, melt the butter in a skillet and whisk in the flour. Cook for 2 to 3 minutes or until light brown, whisking constantly. Whisk in the tomato paste and cook for 1 to 2 minutes. Whisk in the broth gradually. Add the bay leaf and simmer for 20 minutes. Pour through a strainer into a bowl, discarding the bay leaf. Serve with the beef Wellingtons.

MAKES 8 SERVINGS

"Cooking done with care is an act of love."
—Craig Claiborne

HOT HERBED CHICKEN SANDWICH

For the herb butter, combine the parsley, basil, chives and garlic in a food processor and process to mince. Add the pecans, butter, salt, pepper and wine and process to grind the pecans. Add the shallots and process to combine.

For the sandwich, cut 3/4 inch from the top of the bread using a sharp knife. Scoop out the soft interior to form a shell, reserving the shell and the bread. Grind the bread in a food processor; you should have about 2 1/2 cups.

Coat the inside of the bread shell with some of the herbed butter. Arrange half of the mushrooms and chicken in the shell. Season with salt and pepper. Top with a layer of the herb butter and half the bread crumbs. Repeat the layers. Replace the bread top. Sprinkle the wine over the top. Bake on a baking sheet in a preheated 400-degree oven for 1 hour. Let stand for 5 minutes; cut into wedges to serve.

MAKES 6 TO 8 SERVINGS

Herb Butter
1/2 cup parsley
1/2 cup fresh basil leaves
1/2 cup chopped chives
3 garlic cloves
1/4 cup pecan pieces
3/4 cup (1 1/2 sticks) unsalted
    butter, softened
1/2 teaspoon salt
1/2 teaspoon pepper
2 tablespoons dry white wine
2 chopped shallots

Sandwich
1 large round loaf country bread,
    about 12 inches in diameter
8 ounces button mushrooms, sliced
1 3/4 pounds chicken breasts,
    cooked and cubed
1/4 cup dry vermouth

According to the 1880 census, Germans constituted one-third of the San Antonio population. Strong advocates of education, the German community operated the German-English School for its children from 1858 to 1897. Today, these historic buildings serve as a hotel conference center.

CHICKEN DUMPLINGS

6 ounces cream cheese with chives
1/4 cup (1/2 stick) butter, softened
1/8 teaspoon pepper
2 cups chopped cooked chicken
1 small can sliced mushrooms
2 (8-count) cans crescent
roll dough
6 tablespoons butter, melted
2/3 cup herb-seasoned stuffing mix,
crushed to fine crumbs
1/2 cup chopped nuts
1 (10-ounce) can cream of
chicken soup
1 tablespoon sherry, or to taste

Beat the cream cheese, butter and pepper in a bowl until smooth. Add the chicken and mushrooms and mix well. Separate the dough into 16 triangles. Spread each triangle with a small amount of the chicken mixture. Roll to enclose the filling. Pour the melted butter into a shallow bowl. Mix the stuffing mix and nuts on waxed paper or a plate. Dip each dumpling into the melted butter, and then roll in the stuffing mixture. Arrange on a baking sheet and bake in a preheated 375-degree oven for 30 minutes. Mix the soup with the sherry in a small saucepan and heat through, stirring to blend. Serve with the dumplings.

MAKES 8 SERVINGS

HOT CHICKEN SALAD

2 to 2 1/2 cups chopped
cooked chicken
1 (8-ounce) can water chestnuts
1 pimento, diced
1/2 cup slivered almonds, toasted
1/2 cup sliced mushrooms
2 tablespoons lemon juice
1 1/2 cups mayonnaise
Salt and pepper to taste
1/2 cup (2 ounces) shredded
Cheddar cheese
1/2 cup French-fried onions

Mix the chicken, water chestnuts, pimento, almonds, mushrooms, lemon juice and mayonnaise in a bowl. Season with salt and pepper. Spoon into a greased baking dish. Top with the cheese and onions. Bake in a preheated 325-degree oven for 15 minutes or until golden brown.

MAKES 6 SERVINGS

"Laughter is brightest where food is."
—Irish proverb

TOUCH OF SPRING CASSEROLE

Sauté the leeks and asparagus in the butter in a skillet for for 5 to 6 minutes until tender-crisp. Add the hash brown potatoes, pepper strips, salt and dill weed and mix well. Spoon into a 9×13-inch baking dish sprayed with nonstick cooking spray. Beat the eggs and half-and-half in a bowl. Add half the cheese and mix well. Pour over the vegetable mixture. Sprinkle with remaining cheese. Chill, covered with foil, for 8 hours or overnight. Bake in a preheated 350-degree oven for 45 minutes. Uncover and bake for 20 to 25 minutes longer until the center is set. Let stand for 10 minutes before serving.

MAKES 9 SERVINGS

2 leeks, cut into quarters and sliced (about 2 cups)
8 ounces fresh asparagus spears, trimmed and cut into 1-inch pieces
2 tablespoons butter
5 cups frozen Southern-style hash brown potatoes
1/2 cup roasted red pepper strips
1 teaspoon salt
1 teaspoon dried dill weed
8 eggs
1 pint half-and-half
4 ounces fresh Parmesan cheese, finely shredded

HAM AND CHEESE ROLLS

Remove the rolls from the package in one piece. Slice into halves horizontally. Layer the ham and cheese on the bottom half. Replace with the top half. Reassemble in a 9×13-inch baking pan. Cut through the rolls to separate. Mix the remaining ingredients in a bowl. Brush over the rolls, allowing the excess to flow between the rolls. Bake in a preheated 350-degree oven for 15 to 20 minutes. Cover with foil if rolls seem to be browning too quickly.

MAKES 24 SERVINGS

2 packages Pepperidge Farm dinner rolls
2 to 3 ounces ham, sliced
8 ounces Swiss cheese, sliced
1/2 cup (1 stick) margarine, melted
1 tablespoon Worcestershire sauce
1 teaspoon prepared mustard
1 1/2 tablespoons poppy seeds
2 tablespoons onion flakes

APPLE RAISIN QUICHE

1 unbaked (9-inch) pie pastry

1/2 cup raisins

2 teaspoons cinnamon

1/4 cup firmly packed light brown sugar

3 Granny Smith apples, peeled, cored and thinly sliced

3 eggs

1 cup heavy whipping cream

12 ounces Monterey Jack cheese, shredded

Fit the pastry into a pie plate. Prick the bottom and side with a fork. Line snugly with a piece of foil. Bake in a preheated 400-degree oven for 6 minutes. Remove the foil and bake for 10 minutes longer. Remove from the oven.

Mix the raisins, cinnamon and brown sugar in a small bowl. Arrange half the apple slices over the pie crust. Top with the raisin mixture. Repeat the layers. Beat the eggs and cream in a small bowl. Pour the egg mixture over the layers. Top with the cheese. Bake for 1 hour or until the top is brown and the apples are tender. Cool for 10 minutes before slicing.

MAKES 6 TO 8 SERVINGS

COOL CUCUMBER SOUP WITH DILL CREAM

1 cup half-and-half

4 cucumbers peeled, seeded and chopped

2 green onions, sliced

1 tablespoon lemon juice

1 cup half-and-half

2 cups sour cream

1/2 teaspoon salt

1/2 teaspoon hot red pepper sauce

1/2 cup sour cream

1 tablespoon chopped fresh dill weed

Process 1 cup half-and-half, the cucumbers, green onions and lemon juice in a blender or food processor until smooth, stopping to scrape down the side. Combine the cucumber mixture, 1 cup half-and-half, 2 cups sour cream, the salt and hot sauce in a bowl and mix well. Chill, covered, for 8 hours. Blend 1/2 cup sour cream and the dill weed in a bowl. Ladle the soup into bowls. Top each serving with a small amount of the sour cream mixture. Garnish with fresh sprigs of dill weed.

MAKES 4 TO 6 SERVINGS

COOL SUNSET SOUP

Sauté the leeks in the butter in a large saucepan for 4 minutes. Add the carrots and sauté for 5 minutes longer. Add the broth and simmer for 25 minutes. Purée the mixture in batches in a food processor. Chill in the refrigerator.

To serve, whisk in the lemon juice and cilantro. Season with salt and pepper. Ladle into cups or bowls and top each serving with a dollop of sour cream and one cilantro sprig.

MAKES 6 SERVINGS

1 1/2 cups chopped leeks, white parts only
5 tablespoons unsalted butter, melted
3 cups chopped carrots
5 cups chicken broth
1 tablespoon fresh lemon juice
1/4 cup minced fresh cilantro
Salt and freshly ground pepper to taste
1/2 cup sour cream
6 sprigs fresh cilantro

SHRIMP OR LOBSTER BISQUE

Combine the chicken soup, tomato soup, onion, nutmeg and cream in a saucepan. Cook over medium heat until warm, stirring constantly; do not allow to boil. Stir in the shrimp and sherry. Serve in warmed soup bowls with oyster crackers.

MAKES 6 SERVINGS

1 (10-ounce) can cream of chicken soup
1 (10-ounce) can tomato soup
1 tablespoon grated onion
3/4 teaspoon nutmeg
1 cup light cream
1 (6-ounce) can shrimp or lobster, or 3/4 cup fresh shrimp or chopped lobster
1/4 cup dry sherry

"A first-rate soup is more creative than a second-rate painting."
—Abraham Maslov

83

BASIL AND TOMATO SALAD

Garlic Dijon Dressing

*2 tablespoons extra-virgin
olive oil*
1/2 cup red wine vinegar
*2 tablespoons Dijon or
Creole mustard*
1 teaspoon salt
1 teaspoon freshly ground pepper
2 garlic cloves, minced
1 cup extra-virgin olive oil

Salad

5 heads red leaf lettuce, torn
8 large tomatoes, cut into wedges
*4 (14-ounce) cans hearts of
palm, drained and
cut into rounds*
18 fresh basil leaves, chopped
*8 ounces Roquefort cheese,
crumbled*

For the dressing, combine 2 tablespoons olive oil, the vinegar, Dijon mustard, salt, pepper and garlic in a bowl. Whisk in 1 cup olive oil in a thin stream until incorporated.

For the salad, combine the lettuce, tomatoes, hearts of palm and basil in a salad bowl. Pour the dressing over the salad and toss to combine. Sprinkle with the cheese.

MAKES 20 SERVINGS

After the 100-year flood of 1921, the community realized the San Antonio River needed to be tamed before it could be beautified. Protected today by a series of floodgates, dams, and tunnels, the Paseo del Rio, or River Walk, has become the top tourist attraction in Texas.

CRISPY FRIED SHRIMP SALAD

For the shrimp, combine the cornstarch, flour, salt, baking powder, sugar and pepper in a large bowl and mix well. Whisk in the buttermilk and club soda to form a thick batter. Dip the shrimp into the batter. Fry in hot canola oil until golden brown.

For the salad, toss the spinach and vinaigrette in a large salad bowl. Divide the salad among six salad plates. Top each with the orange segments, fried shrimp, almonds and coconut.

MAKES 6 SERVINGS

Shrimp

1 cup cornstarch

1/2 cup all-purpose flour

1/2 teaspoon salt

1 teaspoon baking powder

1 teaspoon sugar

1/2 teaspoon pepper

1 cup buttermilk

1/4 cup club soda

2 pounds shrimp, peeled, deveined and patted dry

Canola oil for frying

Salad

2 pounds fresh baby spinach, rinsed, dried and trimmed

Raspberry vinaigrette dressing

24 ounces mandarin oranges, drained

3 cups thinly sliced red onions

2/3 cup sliced almonds, toasted

1 cup flaked coconut, toasted

"My wife and I had the good fortune of living in the magnificent Pershing House located at Fort Sam Houston, America's most history-filled post. The official inventory lists 934 historic structures—nine times as many as Colonial Williamsburg. Fort Sam is a national treasure that incorporates history, tradition, and valued memories for soldiers and civilians alike."
—Neal T. Jaco,
Lieutenant General (retired),
United States Army

ORANGE AND ALMOND BISCOTTI

2 cups all-purpose flour
1 cup sugar
1 teaspoon baking soda
1/4 teaspoon salt
2 eggs
1 egg yolk
1 teaspoon vanilla extract
1 tablespoon freshly grated orange zest
1 1/2 cups whole almonds, lightly toasted

Combine the flour, sugar, baking soda and salt in a bowl. Whisk the eggs, egg yolk, vanilla and orange zest in a medium bowl. Add to the dry ingredients, beating until a dough forms. Add the almonds and mix well. Turn onto a floured surface and knead several times. Divide into two portions. Roll each portion into a 2×12-inch log. Arrange on a greased baking sheet and flatten slightly. Bake in a preheated 300-degree oven for 50 minutes. Cool for 10 minutes and cut into slices diagonally. Arrange the slices cut side down on a baking sheet. Bake for 15 minutes longer. Cool. Store in an airtight container.

MAKES 30 SERVINGS

ORANGE PECAN SCONES

2 cups self-rising flour
1/2 cup sugar
2 teaspoons grated orange zest
1/3 cup butter
1/2 cup buttermilk
1/4 cup fresh orange juice
1/2 cup chopped toasted pecans
1 teaspoon vanilla extract
Sugar for topping

Combine the flour, sugar and orange zest in a bowl and mix well. Cut in the butter with a pastry blender until the mixture is crumbly. Add the buttermilk, orange juice, pecans and vanilla and mix just until moistened. Turn the dough out onto a lightly floured surface. Knead 3 or 4 times. Divide the dough into two portions. Pat each portion into a 7-inch circle and place on a lightly greased baking sheet. Cut each circle into eight wedges. Sprinkle evenly with additional sugar. Bake in a preheated 425-degree oven for 12 to 14 minutes or until golden brown.

MAKES 16 SERVINGS

BEST-EVER BANANA BREAD

Beat the butter and sugar in a bowl until light and fluffy. Add the eggs one at a time, beating well after each addition. Sift together the flour, baking soda and salt. Add to the butter mixture alternately with the bananas, beating only until the mixture is blended; do not overmix. Fold in the pecans. Divide the batter evenly between two loaf pans sprayed with nonstick cooking spray. Bake in a preheated 350-degree oven or until a tester inserted in the center comes out with just a few crumbs attached. Cool before slicing. Bread improves after storing tightly wrapped for 2 to 3 days.

MAKES 2 LOAVES

1 cup (2 sticks) butter, softened
2 cups sugar
4 eggs
2 1/4 cups all-purpose flour
2 teaspoons baking soda
1 teaspoon salt
6 bananas, mashed
1 cup pecans, toasted and chopped

LEMON TEA BREAD

Beat the butter, 1 cup sugar and lemon zest in a bowl until light and fluffy. Beat in the eggs. Sift the flour and baking powder together. Add to the butter mixture alternately with the milk. Fold in the walnuts. Spoon into a greased loaf pan. Bake in a preheated 375-degree oven for 35 minutes. Combine 1/4 cup sugar, the lemon juice and remaining lemon zest in a small bowl, stirring until smooth. Drizzle over the hot bread. Let the bread cool in the pan for 10 minutes; remove from the pan to cool completely.

MAKES 1 LOAF

1/2 cup (1 stick) butter
1 cup granulated sugar
Grated zest of 1 lemon
2 eggs, beaten
1 1/2 cups all-purpose flour
1 teaspoon baking powder
1/2 cup milk
1/2 cup walnuts, chopped
1/4 cup confectioners' sugar
Juice and grated zest of
*   1 large lemon*

LEMONY FRUIT CREPES

Crepes

1¹/2 cups all-purpose flour

1 tablespoon sugar

¹/2 teaspoon baking powder

¹/2 teaspoon salt

2 cups milk

2 eggs

¹/2 teaspoon vanilla extract

2 tablespoons butter, melted

Filling

1 cup lemon chiffon yogurt

2 teaspoons grated lemon zest

1 teaspoon sugar

2 teaspoons rum

Strawberries, cut into
bite-size pieces

Bananas, cut into bite-size pieces

Pineapple chunks

For the crepes, combine the flour, sugar, baking powder and salt in a large bowl and mix well. Add the milk, eggs, vanilla and butter, beating until smooth.

Butter an 8- to 10-inch crepe pan or skillet. Heat over medium-low heat. Pour in ¹/4 cup of the batter and tilt the pan so the batter covers the bottom evenly. Cook until golden brown. Turn and cook the other side. Repeat until all the batter is used.

For the filling, combine the yogurt, lemon zest, sugar and rum in a large bowl and mix well. Stir in strawberries, bananas and pineapple.

Spoon 1¹/2 tablespoons of the filling into the center of each crepe. Fold the sides over the filling to enclose. Garnish each serving with whipped cream, mint leaves, pieces of fruit or hot fruit preserves.

MAKES 8 SERVINGS

"I feel a recipe is only a theme, which an intelligent cook can play with..."
—Madame Benoit

PINK POACHED PEARS

Combine the raspberries and apple juice in a large saucepan. Bring to a boil; reduce the heat. Simmer for about 5 minutes. Strain into a bowl, pressing hard on the solids to extract the juice. Discard the solids. Stir the honey into the juice mixture.

Layer the pear halves cut sides up in the saucepan. Add the juice mixture. Simmer for 10 minutes or just until the pears are tender. Remove the pears from the saucepan and arrange in a baking dish. Sprinkle with the cinnamon and nutmeg. Add the sugar to the juice mixture, stirring to dissolve. Pour over the pear halves. Chill, covered, for 8 hours or overnight.

To serve as a salad, arrange the pear halves on lettuce-lined serving plates. Combine the cream cheese, pecans and mayonnaise in a small bowl and mix well. Spoon a small amount of the filling mixture into the center of each pear half.

To serve as a side dish, serve cold from the baking dish.

To serve as dessert, place a pear half in a dessert dish and top with a small amount of the juice mixture. Serve with whipped cream and a sprig of mint, if desired.

MAKES 4 TO 6 SERVINGS

1/2 cup fresh or frozen raspberries

2 cups apple juice

1 tablespoon honey

4 firm Bartlett or Anjou pears, peeled, cored and halved

1/4 teaspoon cinnamon

1/4 teaspoon nutmeg

2 tablespoons sugar

1/4 teaspoon almond extract

Salad Option

Lettuce leaves

3 ounces cream cheese, softened

1/4 cup pecans, toasted

1 tablespoon mayonnaise

SWEETWATER STRAWBERRY SHORTBREAD

1/2 cup (1 stick) butter, softened
1/4 cup packed brown sugar
1 cup chopped walnuts or pecans
1 cup all-purpose flour
1 cup whipping cream
1 teaspoon vanilla extract
1/4 cup granulated sugar
1/4 cup packed brown sugar
4 cups chopped strawberries,
drained

Beat the butter, 1/4 cup brown sugar, walnuts and flour in a bowl until a dough forms. Press the dough into a 9-inch springform pan. Bake in a preheated 350-degree oven for 25 minutes; cool.

Beat the cream, vanilla, granulated sugar and 1/4 cup brown sugar in a bowl until light and fluffy. Fold in the strawberries. Spread over the shortbread crust. Chill for several hours. Remove the side of the pan and serve. May be frozen; thaw before serving.

MAKES 10 TO 12 SERVINGS

PUMPKIN DIP

16 ounces cream cheese, softened
1 (16-ounce) package
confectioners' sugar
1 (15-ounce) can pumpkin
2 teaspoons cinnamon
1/2 teaspoon nutmeg
21/2 (14-ounce) packages
gingersnaps

Beat the cream cheese, confectioners' sugar, pumpkin, cinnamon and nutmeg in a large bowl until smooth. Chill for 30 minutes. Spoon into a serving dish and surround with the gingersnaps.

MAKES ABOUT 24 SERVINGS

Although the pumpkin has been called many names, beginning with the Greek term "pepon," American colonists provided the current name. Native Americans not only roasted and ate strips of the pumpkin, they also dried pumpkin rinds and wove them into mats.

THE ANTIQUE ROSE EMPORIUM

*For individuals seeking a source of old rose varieties,
or information about them, the Antique Rose Emporium
provides the service they need. Located on Cibolo Creek,
the Antique Rose Emporium utilizes display gardens
to demonstrate how perennials, herbs, and native plants
can be incorporated into garden designs. In addition,
the Emporium has developed specific areas of its property
for use by the public for special occasions.*

PISTACHIO AND DRIED CRANBERRY BISCOTTI

2¼ cups all-purpose flour
1 cup sugar
½ teaspoon baking powder
½ teaspoon salt
6 tablespoons butter,
cut into small pieces
2 eggs
1 teaspoon vanilla extract
1 cup unsalted pistachios,
coarsely chopped
3 tablespoons dried cranberries

Combine the flour, sugar, baking powder and salt in a large bowl and mix well. Cut in the butter with a pastry blender until the mixture resembles coarse crumbs. Beat in the eggs until blended. Stir in the vanilla. Fold in the pistachios and cranberries; do not overmix.

Divide the dough in half and shape each half into a 2×12-inch log. Chill, wrapped in plastic wrap, for 30 minutes or longer. Place on a cookie sheet and flatten each log slightly. Bake in a preheated 375-degree oven for 20 minutes or until the edges begin to brown. Cool for 10 minutes. Reduce the oven temperature to 325 degrees.

Place the logs on a cutting board and cut diagonally into ½-inch slices. Arrange the slices cut side down on a cookie sheet in a single layer and bake for 15 minutes longer. Cool completely and store in airtight containers.

MAKES 35 BISCOTTI

Biscotti, an Italian cookie, is first baked in a roll, then cut into slices for a second baking. Their firm, crunchy texture and assorted flavors make biscotti a tasty accompaniment to cappuccino.

STRAWBERRIES AND CREAMY VANILLA SAUCE

Place the strawberries in a shallow bowl. Add the liqueur and mix to combine. Chill, covered, in the refrigerator.

Combine the cream cheese, confectioners' sugar and vanilla in a blender. Process until well blended. Pour in the cream and continue mixing until well-blended. Serve the sauce over the strawberries.

MAKES 4 SERVINGS

1 pint fresh strawberries
1 cup Cointreau
8 ounces cream cheese, softened
8 ounces confectioners' sugar
1 teaspoon vanilla extract
1 cup heavy whipping cream

Garnishes enhance the presentation of foods. Although they are not always eaten, garnishes should be edible and fresh, and their color should complement the food and table decor.

SAVORY
SIDE DISHES

NOW SERVING: I'M IN CHARGE

The **I'm in Charge** project introduces important safety information to elementary students in participating San Antonio school districts. Trained Assistance League® volunteers go into classrooms and show a safety video, followed by a discussion about personal safety. Each child is given a safety booklet to take home. During the week of September 11, kindergarten and first-grade students in participating schools are given crayons and coloring books with similar safety information. Children are taught how to avoid dangerous situations and what to do if they find themselves in harm's way.

SUMMER'S END

Williamsburg Cheese Straws page 20
Cool Sunset Soup page 83
Five-Spice Scallops page 139
New Potatoes with Thyme page 101
Spinach Madeleine page 103
Heavenly Angel Lemon Pie page 145
Coffee or Tea
Pinot Grigio or
other Italian white wine

A NOTABLE DINNER

Blue Cheese "Frosted" Pears page 14
Garlic Shrimp page 24
Cream of Brie Soup with
Toasty Croutons page 55
Hearts of Palm Salad with Basil
and Garlic Dressing page 66
Tournedos Diables page 119
South-of-the-Border
Green Beans page 100
Yellow Squash Puff page 105
Foccacia Bread with
Dipping Oil
Praline-Crusted Cheesecake page 142
Cabernet Sauvignon
Irish Coffee

ARTICHOKE CASSEROLE

1 large Spanish onion, sliced
Melted butter for sautéing
2 or 3 (9-ounce) packages frozen
artichoke hearts
1/2 cup mayonnaise
1/2 cup grated Parmesan cheese
2 (14-ounce) cans whole tomatoes
Salt and pepper to taste
1 1/2 teaspoons chopped fresh basil
1 1/2 teaspoons fresh oregano leaves
6 ounces shredded Monterey
Jack cheese

Sauté the onions in butter in a skillet until tender. Cook the artichokes according to the package directions. Combine the mayonnaise and Parmesan cheese in a small bowl and mix well. Layer the onions, artichoke hearts, mayonnaise mixture and tomatoes in a casserole. Sprinkle with the salt, pepper, basil and oregano. Top with the Monterey Jack cheese. Bake in a preheated 350-degree oven for 30 minutes.

MAKES 6 TO 8 SERVINGS

BROCCOLI CASSEROLE

4 slices bacon
8 ounces cream cheese
1/4 cup chopped onion
1/4 cup (1/2 stick) butter, melted
2 tablespoons all-purpose flour
Salt to taste
1/2 cup water
2 (16-ounce) packages frozen
chopped broccoli, cooked
and drained
1 (5-ounce) can water
chestnuts, sliced
3 eggs, beaten
Buttered bread crumbs

Cook the bacon in a skillet until crisp; drain and crumble. Cut the cream cheese into cubes. Sauté the onion in the butter in a skillet until tender. Stir in the flour and salt. Add the water and cook until thickened, stirring constantly. Add the cream cheese and cook until melted, stirring frequently. Add the bacon, broccoli and water chestnuts and mix well. Remove from the heat. (Recipe may be prepared in advance to this point and stored in the refrigerator.) Stir in the eggs and pour into a greased baking dish. Top with bread crumbs. Bake in a preheated 325-degree oven for 30 minutes or until set.

MAKES 8 SERVINGS

BLACK-EYED PEA SALAD TEXAS STYLE

Soak the peas in water to cover in a bowl overnight; drain. Rinse and drain again. Combine the peas with fresh water to cover in a saucepan and bring to a boil. Reduce the heat and simmer, covered, for 1 hour or until tender but not mushy; do not overcook.

Drain the peas; rinse and drain again. Pour into a large bowl. Add the bell pepper, pimento, onions, garlic, jalapeño chiles, salt and pepper. Add the salad dressing, tossing to coat. Serve hot or cold.

MAKES ABOUT 4 CUPS

8 ounces dried black-eyed peas
1 cup chopped green bell pepper
1/4 cup chopped pimento
1 cup chopped onion
1/2 cup finely chopped
    green onions
2 tablespoons chopped garlic
1/4 cup finely chopped
    jalapeño chiles
Salt and pepper to taste
1 cup Italian salad dressing

Great for serving on New Year's Day to bring a year of good luck! Prepare the day before and refrigerate, if desired.

CAULIFLOWER AU GRATIN

*1 head cauliflower, broken
into florets
Pinch of salt
2 cups milk
1 cup cream
3 tablespoons butter
1/4 cup all-purpose flour
Salt and pepper to taste
Freshly grated nutmeg to taste
1 cup (4 ounces) grated Gruyère
or shredded Swiss cheese*

Cook the cauliflower with a pinch of salt in water in a saucepan for 6 to 8 minutes or until tender. Drain, reserving the cooking liquid; cool.

Heat the milk and cream in a saucepan just to boiling. Melt the butter in a saucepan. Whisk in the flour and cook for 1 minute, whisking constantly. Whisk in the hot milk mixture. Cook until thickened, stirring constantly. Season with salt, pepper and nutmeg. Thin with some of the reserved cooking liquid if needed.

Arrange the cauliflower in a greased 2-quart casserole. Toss with 1/4 cup of the cheese. Pour the sauce over the cauliflower. Top with the remaining 3/4 cup cheese. Bake in a preheated 375-degree oven for 30 to 40 minutes until bubbly and brown.

You may roast the cauliflower rather than boiling or steaming it. Place the cauliflower in an ovenproof dish and toss with 2 tablespoons olive oil and salt and pepper to taste. Roast in a preheated 350-degree oven for 30 minutes.

MAKES 6 SERVINGS

Made from cow's milk, Gruyère cheese makes a simple, satisfying snack served with fruit and crackers. Its sweet but nutty flavor is also a suitable addition to vegetable dishes.

CORN PUDDING

Combine the sour cream, butter and eggs and beat until well blended. Stir in the muffin mix, cream-style corn and undrained whole kernel corn. Pour into a greased 9×13-inch baking pan. Bake in a preheated 350-degree oven for 35 to 40 minutes or until set.

MAKES 8 TO 10 SERVINGS

1 cup sour cream

1/2 cup (1 stick) butter or margarine, melted

2 eggs

1 (8-ounce) package corn muffin mix

1 (16-ounce) can cream-style corn

1 (16-ounce) can whole kernel corn

STUFFED EGGPLANT

Cut off one side of the eggplant and remove the pulp, leaving a 1/2-inch shell. Chop the pulp and set aside. Combine 1/2 cup water and the salt in a saucepan. Add the chopped eggplant and cook for 10 minutes or until tender. Drain well. Sauté the onion in 1 tablespoon butter in a skillet until tender but not brown. Add the chopped eggplant, soup, parsley, Worcestershire sauce and cracker crumbs, reserving 2 tablespoons of the crumbs for topping. Spoon into the eggplant shell. Place the stuffed eggplant in a greased 6×10-inch baking dish. Dot with butter and sprinkle with the reserved cracker crumbs. Pour 1 cup water into the dish. Bake in a preheated 375-degree oven for 1 hour or until the eggplant shell is tender and the filling is hot.

MAKES 4 TO 6 SERVINGS

1 large eggplant

1/2 cup water

1/2 teaspoon salt

1/4 cup chopped onion

1 tablespoon butter

1/2 (10-ounce) can cream of mushroom soup

1 tablespoon parsley

1 tablespoon Worcestershire sauce

1 cup butter cracker crumbs

Butter

1 cup water

SOUTH-OF-THE-BORDER GREEN BEANS

6 slices bacon
1/2 onion, chopped
1/2 cup chopped celery
3 cups cooked green beans
1 (8-ounce) can tomato sauce
1 teaspoon Worcestershire sauce
Salt and pepper to taste
1/2 cup buttered bread crumbs

Sauté the bacon, onion and celery in a skillet until the bacon is brown and crisp; drain and crumble the bacon. Mix the green beans, tomato sauce, Worcestershire sauce, salt and pepper in a bowl. Add the bacon and onion mixture to the green bean mixture and mix well. Spoon into a greased 1 1/2-quart baking dish. Top with the bread crumbs. Bake, uncovered, in a preheated 375-degree oven for 20 minutes.

MAKES 4 TO 6 SERVINGS

GREEN BEAN SALAD WITH SOUR CREAM DRESSING

2 flats anchovy fillets,
drained, or 1 tube
anchovy paste
1 cup mayonnaise
3/4 cup (or more) wine vinegar
2 cups sour cream
Chopped chives or green onions
Cayenne pepper and salt to taste
8 to 10 (14-ounce) cans whole
Blue Lake green beans

Combine the anchovies, mayonnaise and vinegar in a blender and process to blend. Fold the mixture into the sour cream in a bowl. Add the chives, cayenne pepper and salt. Taste the mixture and add additional vinegar if needed for the desired tartness.

Drain the green beans well. Combine with the sour cream dressing in a bowl. Chill thoroughly.

MAKES 20 SERVINGS

"The secret of good cooking is, having a love of it..."
—*James Beard*

NEW POTATOES WITH THYME

Whisk the olive oil, kosher salt, thyme and vinegar in a small bowl. Combine with the potatoes in a large bowl or sealable plastic bag. Toss to coat evenly. Spread in an even layer on a baking sheet or roasting pan. Drizzle the marinade over the potatoes. Roast in a preheated 425-degree oven for 50 minutes until tender and slightly brown.

MAKES 6 TO 8 SERVINGS

3 tablespoons olive oil
2 teaspoons kosher salt
1 teaspoon dried thyme
3 tablespoons cider vinegar
2 pounds new potatoes,
    cut into quarters

DAY-AHEAD MASHED POTATOES

Peel the potatoes and cook in boiling salted water in a large saucepan until tender. Drain well. Mash the potatoes in a bowl. Whip in the cream cheese, 1 tablespoon butter, salt, pepper and sour cream gradually. Spoon into a 9×13-inch baking dish. Dot with butter and sprinkle with seasoned salt. Refrigerate until ready to heat through and serve.

MAKES 8 TO 10 SERVINGS

8 to 10 potatoes
8 ounces cream cheese,
    cut into pieces
1 tablespoon butter
1 teaspoon salt
1 teaspoon pepper
1/2 cup to 1 cup sour cream
1 tablespoon butter,
    cut into pieces
Seasoned salt or paprika

BOURBON SWEET POTATOES
WITH STREUSEL TOPPING

4 or 5 sweet potatoes, cooked
and peeled
1 cup granulated sugar
3 eggs
1 (5-ounce) can evaporated milk
1 teaspoon vanilla extract
2 tablespoons bourbon
1 cup pecans, chopped
1 cup packed brown sugar
1 cup all-purpose flour
1/2 cup (1 stick) butter, softened

Mash the cooked sweet potatoes in a bowl. Add the granulated sugar, eggs, evaporated milk, vanilla and bourbon and mix well. Spoon into a greased 9×13-inch baking dish or two round baking dishes.

Combine the pecans, brown sugar, flour and butter in a bowl or a food processor and mix well. Sprinkle over the sweet potato mixture. Bake in a preheated 350-degree oven for 40 minutes.

MAKES 6 TO 8 SERVINGS

You can bake the whole casserole ahead of time and freeze it. Thaw it and reheat for a quick holiday side dish.

GREAT PUMPKIN

Wash the pumpkin. Cut off the top and reserve. Scoop out the seeds. Combine the apples, raisins, pecans, sugar, lemon juice, cinnamon, nutmeg and butter in a bowl and mix well. Spoon the mixture into the pumpkin shell. Replace the top. Place the pumpkin on a lightly greased baking sheet. Bake in a preheated 350-degree oven for 1 hour and 15 minutes. Remove the top and spoon sour cream over the stuffing. Serve hot or cold.

MAKES 4 TO 6 SERVINGS

1 small pumpkin, about 7 inches in diameter
2 cups chopped peeled apples
1 cup raisins
1 cup chopped pecans
1/3 cup granulated sugar or light brown sugar
1 teaspoon lemon juice
1/4 teaspoon cinnamon
1/4 teaspoon nutmeg
1 tablespoon butter, softened
Sour cream

SPINACH MADELEINE

Cook the spinach according to the package directions. Drain, reserving 1/2 cup of the cooking liquid. Sauté the onion in the margarine in a skillet until tender. Stir in the flour. Add the reserved cooking liquid and evaporated milk. Cook until smooth and thickened, stirring constantly. Add the pepper, garlic salt, salt, Worcestershire sauce and cheese. Cook until the cheese melts, stirring constantly. Combine the sauce with the spinach in a bowl. Pour into a 2-quart baking dish. Top with buttered bread crumbs. Bake in a preheated 350-degree oven for 30 minutes or until bubbly.

MAKES 8 SERVINGS

2 (10-ounce) packages frozen chopped spinach
2 tablespoons chopped onion
1/4 cup (1/2 stick) margarine, melted
2 tablespoons all-purpose flour
1/2 cup evaporated milk
1/2 teaspoon pepper
3/4 teaspoon garlic salt
3/4 teaspoon salt
1 teaspoon Worcestershire sauce
1 (6-ounce) package jalapeño cheese, cut into small pieces
Buttered bread crumbs

103

LUCHOW'S POTATO PANCAKES

2 pounds potatoes (about 6)
1/2 onion, grated
2 tablespoons all-purpose flour
2 eggs, beaten
1 1/2 teaspoons salt
1/4 teaspoon pepper
1/4 teaspoon grated nutmeg
2 tablespoons minced parsley
3 to 4 tablespoons butter
4 slices bacon, crisp-cooked
and crumbled

Wash and peel potatoes. Cover with cold water; drain. Grate immediately and drain the liquid that collects on the grated potatoes. Add the onion and mix well. Add the flour, eggs, salt, pepper, nutmeg and parsley and mix well. Heat the butter on a griddle or in a large frying pan.

Spoon the potato mixture onto the hot griddle. Cook 3 or 4 pancakes at a time until brown and crisp on both sides. Top with the bacon.

MAKES 6 SERVINGS

SQUASH CASSEROLE

4 large yellow squash or zucchini,
chopped, (about 6 cups)
1 large onion, chopped
2 tablespoons butter, melted
1 garlic clove, minced
1 egg, beaten
1/2 cup sour cream
1 teaspoon salt
1/2 teaspoon pepper
1 cup (4 ounces) shredded
Pepper Jack cheese
2 tablespoons butter, melted
1 cup crushed butter crackers

Steam the squash in a steamer until tender. Drain well and mash in a bowl. Sauté the onion in 2 tablespoons butter in a skillet until tender. Stir in the garlic. Add to the squash and mix well.

Combine the egg and sour cream in a bowl and mix well. Stir into the squash mixture. Season with salt and pepper. Add the cheese and mix well. Pour into a greased 8×10-inch baking dish.

Combine 2 tablespoons butter and the cracker crumbs in a bowl. Sprinkle over the squash mixture. Bake in a preheated 350-degree oven until heated through and the topping is brown and crispy.

MAKES 8 SERVINGS

YELLOW SQUASH PUFF

Cook the squash in a small amount of water until tender but not mushy. Drain and mash. Combine with the milk, bread crumbs, salt, onion, pepper, cheese and egg yolks in a large bowl and mix well.

Beat the egg whites in a bowl until soft peaks form and fold into the squash mixture. Spoon into a baking dish sprayed with nonstick cooking spray. Set in a pan of hot water.

Bake in a preheated 350-degree oven for 30 minutes or until set. Recipe may be made a day in advance and also may be doubled.

MAKES 6 SERVINGS

2 pounds yellow crookneck
 squash, sliced
1/2 cup milk
2 cups soft bread crumbs
1 teaspoon salt
1 teaspoon grated onion
1/4 teaspoon pepper
1 cup (4 ounces) shredded sharp
 Cheddar cheese
2 egg yolks
2 egg whites

Versatile yellow squash can be steamed, boiled, baked, or deep fried. When selecting summer squash, choose the smaller, blemish-free specimens. When picking out winter squash, select those that are heavy for their size, with hard, deep-colored rinds free of spots.

VEGETABLE STRUDEL

1/3 cup julienned zucchini
1/3 cup julienned yellow squash
1/3 cup julienned carrots
1/3 cup julienned red bell pepper
1 1/2 tablespoons olive oil
4 ounces fresh spinach,
washed and patted dry
1/4 cup white wine
1/3 cup crumbled feta cheese
Salt and white pepper to taste
10 sheets phyllo dough
3 tablespoons butter, melted

Sauté the zucchini, squash, carrots and bell pepper in the olive oil in a large skillet for 2 minutes. Add the spinach and wine. Cook for 1 minute. Stir in the cheese. Remove from the heat and season with salt and white pepper.

Stack the phyllo sheets and brush with 1 1/2 tablespoons of the butter. Spread the vegetables evenly over the phyllo. Roll to enclose, forming a cylinder. Brush with the remaining 1 1/2 tablespoons butter. Place on a baking sheet. Bake in a preheated 375-degree oven for 25 minutes or until light golden brown. Cut into 8 slices.

MAKES 8 SERVINGS

Strudel, the German word for "whirlpool" or "eddy,"
is a pastry made from layers of thin sheets of dough
filled with various ingredients prior to baking.
Frozen phyllo leaves for strudel can be found in the
frozen food section of most supermarkets.

SPICED PEACHES

Drain the peaches, reserving 1 cup of the syrup. Combine the syrup with the vinegar, sugar, cinnamon stick and cloves in a saucepan and mix well. Bring to a boil and reduce the heat. Simmer, uncovered, for 5 minutes. Add the peach halves and return to a boil. Remove from the heat and cool. Remove the cinnamon stick and cloves. Chill the peaches for 24 hours or longer. Serve cold. This recipe is easily doubled.

MAKES 8 SERVINGS

3 (15-ounce) cans peach halves

1/2 cup vinegar

1/2 cup sugar

1 cinnamon stick

1 heaping teaspoon whole cloves

KILLER CORN BREAD

Beat the sugar and butter in a large bowl until creamy. Stir in the eggs one at a time. Stir in the cheese, cornmeal, flour, baking powder, salt and corn and mix well. Spoon into a greased 9×13-inch baking dish. Bake in a preheated 350-degree oven for 30 minutes or until a tester inserted in the center comes out clean.

MAKES 6 TO 8 SERVINGS

1 cup sugar

1 cup (2 sticks) butter, softened

4 eggs

1 cup (4 ounces) shredded Cheddar cheese

1 cup yellow cornmeal

1 cup all-purpose flour

4 teaspoons baking powder

1/4 teaspoon salt

1 (14-ounce) can cream-style corn

This recipe can be halved and baked in a smaller dish or in muffin cups.

CORN BREAD CASSEROLE

1 pound bacon

3 eggs

1/2 cup sour cream

1 (14-ounce) can sweet corn, drained

1 (14-ounce) can cream-style corn

1 (6-ounce) package corn bread mix

1 bell pepper, chopped

1 bunch green onions, sliced

10 ounces Cheddar cheese, shredded

Salt to taste

1/4 cup (1/2 stick) butter, melted

Fry the bacon in a skillet until crisp; drain and crumble. Combine the eggs, sour cream, sweet corn and cream-style corn in a large bowl and mix well. Add the corn bread mix, bell pepper and green onions and mix well. Add the bacon, cheese and salt and mix well. Pour into a greased 9×13-inch baking pan. Pour the melted butter over the top. Bake in a preheated 350-degree oven for 1 hour or until slightly brown on top.

MAKES 12 SERVINGS

GLORIFIED FRENCH BREAD

1 loaf French bread

1/2 cup (1 stick) butter, softened

1/4 cup mayonnaise (optional)

2 cups (8 ounces) shredded mozzarella cheese

1/2 cup chopped black or green olives

1 teaspoon garlic powder

1 teaspoon onion powder

Split the loaf lengthwise. Spread with the butter and mayonnaise. Sprinkle the cheese, olives, garlic powder and onion powder over the bottom half of the bread. Replace the top. Bake, wrapped in foil, in a preheated 350-degree oven for 10 to 15 minutes or until hot. Cut into slices to serve.

MAKES 8 SERVINGS

FABULOUS CHEESE GRITS

Bring the stock to a boil in a saucepan and gradually stir in the grits. Cook until thickened, stirring constantly. Season with salt and pepper. Add the garlic cheese and mix well. Stir in the eggs, butter and milk. Pour into a greased 9×13-inch baking dish. Sprinkle with the Cheddar cheese and dust with paprika. Bake in a preheated 350-degree oven for 35 to 40 minutes or until hot.

MAKES 8 SERVINGS

6 cups chicken stock

2 cups grits

Salt and pepper to taste

2 (6-ounce) rolls garlic cheese, cut into cubes

4 eggs, lightly beaten

1/2 cup (1 stick) butter

1/2 cup milk

1 cup (4 ounces) shredded Cheddar cheese

Paprika

SWISS CHEESE GRITS CASSEROLE

Bring the milk almost to a boil in a saucepan and gradually stir in the grits. Cook for 3 minutes or until thickened, stirring constantly. Remove from the heat and stir in the butter, Swiss cheese, salt and pepper. Pour into a greased 9×10-inch baking dish. Top with the cornflakes and Parmesan cheese. Bake in a preheated 350-degree oven for 30 minutes.

MAKES 8 SERVINGS

1 quart milk

1 cup grits

1 cup (2 sticks) butter

1 cup (4 ounces) shredded Swiss cheese

1/2 teaspoon salt

1/2 teaspoon pepper

1 cup crushed cornflakes

1/3 cup grated Parmesan cheese

Derived from the Old English word "grytt," grits refers to a coarsely ground grain of any kind. Native Americans first produced corn grits centuries ago.

HILL COUNTRY
CORN BREAD DRESSING

1 large onion, chopped
2 tablespoons vegetable oil
1 (8-ounce) package
corn bread mix
2 bell peppers, cut into halves
1 to 2 tablespoons vegetable oil
1 loaf wheat bread
2 (5-ounce) cans sliced water
chestnuts, drained
and chopped
Tops of 2 bunches green
onions, sliced
1 cup chopped celery
(with leaves)
1/2 cup chopped parsley
2 tablespoons dried sage
8 hard-cooked eggs, chopped
Salt and pepper to taste
4 to 5 (15-ounce) cans
chicken broth

Sauté the onion in 2 tablespoons oil in a cast-iron skillet until tender. Prepare the corn bread mix according to the package directions. Add to the hot onion and mix well. Bake in the skillet according to the package directions. Cool the corn bread and crumble into a large bowl. Sauté the bell pepper in 1 to 2 tablespoons oil in a skillet until tender. Chop the bell pepper.

Remove the heels and crusts from the wheat bread and crumble. Add to the corn bread mixture and mix well. Measure the corn bread mixture. Crumble and add enough of the remaining wheat bread to equal the amount of corn bread mixture. Mix well. Add the bell peppers, water chestnuts, green onions, celery, parsley, sage, eggs, salt and pepper and mix well. Chill, covered, overnight.

When ready to cook, add enough of the broth to just cover the dressing. Spoon into a greased 9×13-inch baking pan. Bake in a preheated 350-degree oven for 2 hours or until the center is firm to the touch.

MAKES 12 SERVINGS

Mission San Juan Capistrano, which was moved by the Spanish from east Texas to its present location in 1756, became a thriving agricultural center whose major service was to provide food for those who lived in the area. Surplus food was sold to markets located to the east, in Louisiana, and to the south, in Coahuila, Mexico.

BAKED PASTA AND GORGONZOLA

Sauté the mushrooms and garlic in the butter in a large skillet for 15 minutes or until the liquid evaporates. Add the sage and 7 cups radicchio and mix well. Remove from the heat and set aside.

Cook the pasta to al dente; drain well. Combine the pasta, Parmesan cheese, Gorgonzola cheese, cream, salt, pepper and mushroom mixture in a large bowl and mix well. Spoon into a greased 9×13-inch baking pan. Bake in a preheated 400-degree oven for 25 minutes or until heated through. Sprinkle with 1 cup radicchio and serve.

MAKES 6 TO 8 SERVINGS

1 pound mushrooms, sliced
3 or 4 garlic cloves, minced
5 tablespoons butter
1/4 cup fresh sage leaves, chopped, or 1 tablespoon dried sage
7 cups shredded radicchio
1 pound penne
2 cups (8 ounces) freshly grated Parmesan cheese
2 cups crumbled Gorgonzola cheese
2 cups light cream
Salt and pepper to taste
1 cup shredded radicchio

Although used mostly for salads to add color and flavor, radicchio provides distinctive flavor to sautéed or baked dishes.

III

MISSION CONCEPCIÓN

*Combining the Moorish elements found in Spanish building design with
Native American influences, Mission Nuestra Señora de la Concepción de Acuna
has been described as a grand representation of Spanish colonial architecture.
Concepción served as the headquarters for the local religious coordinator,
whose mission was to replace the Native American celebrations with Christian
pageantry such as Los Posadas, the reenactment of Christ's birth.*

MEXICAN RICE

Heat the bacon drippings in a saucepan and add the rice. Sauté the rice until brown. Add the tomato, onion, bell pepper, salt, cumin, chili powder, garlic and water and bring to a boil. Reduce the heat and simmer, covered, for 30 minutes. Do not lift the lid!

MAKES 6 TO 8 SERVINGS

2 tablespoons bacon drippings
1 cup rice
1/4 cup chopped fresh tomato
1/2 cup chopped onion
1/4 cup chopped green bell pepper
1 teaspoon salt
1/8 teaspoon cumin
1 1/4 teaspoons chili powder
2 garlic cloves, minced
2 cups water

MUSHROOM RICE

Melt the butter in an ovenproof saucepan or Dutch oven. Add the onion and sauté until tender but not brown. Add the mushrooms and wine. Increase the heat to high and cook until the liquid evaporates and the mixture begins to sizzle. Add the rice and cook for 1 minute, stirring constantly. Stir in the broth and salt. Bake, covered, in a preheated 350-degree oven for 45 minutes. Sprinkle with the cheese and fluff with a fork.

MAKES 6 SERVINGS

1/4 cup (1/2 stick) butter
1/2 cup chopped onion
3/4 cup thinly sliced mushrooms
1/2 cup dry white wine
1 cup rice
2 1/2 cups beef broth or
   chicken broth
1/2 teaspoon salt
2 tablespoons Parmesan cheese

> *"(Rice) is beautiful when...it enters granary bins like a (flood) of seed-pearls. It is beautiful when cooked by a practiced hand, pure white and sweetly fragrant."*
> —Shizuo Tsuji

113

GOURMET WILD RICE

1/3 cup currants

2 tablespoons brandy

2/3 cup wild rice

2 cups chicken broth

2 tablespoons olive oil

1/3 cup pine nuts, toasted

Combine the currants and brandy in a bowl and set aside. Rinse and drain the wild rice in hot water in a bowl. Repeat two more times. Combine the wild rice and broth in a medium saucepan and bring to a boil. Reduce the heat. Simmer, covered, for 45 minutes or until the rice is tender and the liquid is absorbed.

Stir the currant mixture, olive oil and pine nuts into the rice. Fluff with a fork before serving.

MAKES 6 SERVINGS

ORANGE RICE

1/4 cup (1/2 stick) butter

2/3 cup chopped celery

2 tablespoons minced onion

1 1/2 cups water

2 tablespoons grated orange zest

1 cup orange juice,
preferably with pulp

1 teaspoon salt

1/8 teaspoon dried thyme

1 1/2 cups rice

Melt the butter in a large skillet over low heat. Add the celery and onion. Cook until tender but not brown. Stir in the water, orange zest, orange juice, salt and thyme and bring to a boil. Add the rice and mix well. Reduce the heat. Simmer, covered, until the liquid is absorbed. Fluff with a fork before serving.

MAKES 4 SERVINGS

CRANBERRY CHUTNEY

Cook the cranberries in a small amount of water for several minutes or until they pop. Set aside. Heat the jelly with the vinegar, honey and sugar in a saucepan. Simmer until the sugar dissolves, stirring constantly. Add the cranberries, raisins, garlic, cinnamon, allspice, ginger, salt, pepper flakes and pecans and mix well. Let stand for 1 hour for the flavors to blend. You may substitute 1 or 2 garlic cloves for the granulated garlic.

MAKES 6 CUPS

1 pound fresh or frozen cranberries
1 (10-ounce) jar jalapeño jelly
1/4 cup apple cider vinegar
1/2 cup honey
2 cups sugar
1 cup raisins
1 tablespoon granulated garlic
1/2 teaspoon each cinnamon,
    ground allspice, ginger, salt
    and crushed red pepper flakes
2 cups toasted chopped pecans

APRICOT CHUTNEY

Combine all the ingredients in a large heavy saucepan and mix well. Cook over low heat for 45 minutes or until the mixture reaches a jam-like consistency, stirring occasionally. Spoon the mixture into clean sterilized glass jars and top with clean lids. Store in the refrigerator for up to 6 weeks.

MAKES 3 1/2 CUPS

Chutney is a spiced East Indian-style relish or pickle that is used as a condiment or seasoning ingredient. Most chutneys are fruit-based and can contain apricots, plums, peaches, and/or mangoes.

1 pound dried apricots, chopped
1 1/2 cups firmly packed light
    brown sugar
1 cup cider vinegar
1 onion, chopped
1 cup water
1/3 cup golden raisins
2 garlic cloves, finely chopped
2 tablespoons minced peeled
    fresh ginger
1 tablespoon salt
1 teaspoon coriander seeds,
    lightly crushed
1/2 teaspoon (or less)
    cayenne pepper

EXCEPTIONAL ENTREES & DINNER PARTIES

NOW SERVING: DREAMS COME TRUE

Have you ever had a dream? For some elementary students, the dream is of a time when they can select their own clothes.

Operation School Bell® helps this dream become reality for children in grades kindergarten through five who are identified by an agency or school counselor. When they arrive at Assistance League® headquarters, each child receives one-on-one assistance from a volunteer in selecting two new outfits of clothing including socks and underwear, a coat, a personal care kit, a pencil box, a shoe voucher, and a book. In addition, the children are shown the "I'm in Charge" personal safety video and given a safety booklet to take home.

Operation School Bell® also makes the dreams of teachers come true. Through this project, grants for educational enrichment programs are given to local elementary teachers.

RAINY DAY BRIGHTENER	COMPANY'S COMING
Crab Imperial with Whole Grain Crackers page 25	*Won Tons Hawaiian Style* page 16
Orange Chicken page 131	*Pineapple, Banana and Watermelon Kababs with White Sangria* page 31
Vegetable Strudel page 106	*Southwest Salmon Tostada* page 137
Broccoli Salad page 63	*Spinach and Basil Salad* page 70
Pecan Caramel Chocolate Mousse Pie page 144	*Margarita Pie* page 145
Coffee	*Sauvignon Blanc*
Syrah or Shiraz	

BAR K RANCH PRIME RIB

1 tablespoon Worcestershire sauce
1 teaspoon garlic powder
3 tablespoons cracked
black pepper
1 (5-pound) prime rib roast
2 (4-pound) bags rock salt
1/2 cup water

Combine the Worcestershire sauce, garlic powder and black pepper in a small bowl. Rub over the roast. Pour the rock salt 1/2 inch deep into a disposable aluminum pan. Place the roast in the center. Add the remaining rock salt, patting over the entire roast. Sprinkle with the water.

Bake in a preheated 500-degree oven for 12 minutes per pound until a meat thermometer registers 145 degrees for medium-rare, or to the desired degree of doneness.

Crack the salt crust with a hammer. Remove the roast and brush away the rock salt.

MAKES 8 SERVINGS

Mission San José y San Miguel de Aguayo was considered by the Spanish to be the best-fortified structure on the frontier. Later San José Mission became known as the "Queen of Missions" because of its architectural design. Today, its original wooden door and hand-carved "rose window" are tourist favorites.

TOURNEDOS DIABLES

Sprinkle the tenderloin with pepper and garlic salt. Grill over medium-hot coals for 15 minutes on each side or to the desired degree of doneness.

Prepare the rice according to the package directions. Keep warm. Bring the bouillon to a boil in a heavy saucepan. Reduce the heat to a simmer.

Heat the sherry and Cognac in a small saucepan until hot, but not boiling. Remove from the heat, ignite with a match and pour over the bouillon. After the flames die down, add the butter, Dijon mustard, tomato paste, vinegar and garlic powder. Cook over low heat for 15 minutes. Stir in the mushrooms and green onions. Simmer for 5 minutes.

Cut the tenderloin into 1/2-inch slices. Arrange the slices over the rice on a serving platter. Top with the sauce.

MAKES 8 TO 10 SERVINGS

1 (5- to 7-pound) beef tenderloin, trimmed
Coarsely ground pepper and garlic salt to taste
1 (6-ounce) package long grain and wild rice blend
2 cups beef bouillon
1/3 cup sherry
1/4 cup Cognac
2 teaspoons butter
1 tablespoon plus 1 teaspoon Dijon mustard
1 tablespoon tomato paste
1/2 teaspoon vinegar
1/2 teaspoon garlic powder
1 cup sliced fresh mushrooms
1 cup chopped green onions

An old adage advises, "After lunch sit a while, and after dinner walk a mile."

OVEN-BARBECUED BRISKET

1/2 cup liquid smoke

1 teaspoon garlic salt

2 teaspoons celery seeds

1 teaspoon onion salt

1 1/2 teaspoons salt

2 teaspoons pepper

*2 tablespoons
Worcestershire sauce*

*1 (3 1/2- to 4 1/2-pound) beef
brisket, trimmed and square
cut (if you prefer lean brisket)*

*2 cups Smoke and Sugar
Barbecue Sauce*

Combine the liquid smoke, garlic salt, celery seeds, onion salt, salt, pepper and Worcestershire sauce in a bowl. Rub over the brisket. Marinate, covered, in the refrigerator overnight.

Place the brisket in a roasting pan. Bake, covered in heavy-duty foil, in a preheated 250-degree oven for 5 hours. Remove the foil and spread thickly with barbecue sauce. Bake in a preheated 350-degree oven for 1 hour longer. Let stand for 30 minutes and cut into crosswise slices.

MAKES 8 SERVINGS

SMOKE AND SUGAR
BARBECUE SAUCE

1/2 cup (1 stick) butter

5 tablespoons brown sugar

1 tablespoon dry mustard

6 tablespoons liquid smoke

6 tablespoons Worcestershire sauce

5 teaspoons celery seeds

2 cups ketchup

1 cup water

Melt the butter in a saucepan. Add the brown sugar and dry mustard and mix well. Cook until the sugar dissolves, stirring constantly. Stir in the liquid smoke, Worcestershire sauce, celery seeds, ketchup and water. Simmer for 15 minutes.

MAKES ABOUT 5 CUPS

*Use your favorite barbecue sauce for the above brisket,
or try this terrific and easy homemade version.*

STEAK DIANE

Sauté the steaks in the butter in a large skillet over medium-high heat for 1 1/2 minutes on one side. Season with salt and pepper. Turn the steaks and cook for 1 minute longer for medium-rare. Reduce the heat and add the green onions, garlic and mushrooms. Cook for 1 1/2 minutes. Remove from the heat. Remove the steak mixture to an ovenproof plate and keep warm in a preheated 200-degree oven.

Reheat the skillet. Add the brandy. Heat for a few seconds, and then ignite. Tilt the pan away until the flames subside. Add the bouillon, cream and Dijon mustard and mix well. Add the Worcestershire sauce and hot pepper sauce. Cook for 1 to 2 minutes to combine the flavors. Return the steak mixture to the skillet and coat with the sauce. Place the steaks on a serving platter or individual plates. Pour the sauce over the steaks and sprinkle with the parsley.

MAKES 4 SERVINGS

4 (5-ounce) beef tenderloin fillets
2 tablespoons butter, melted
Salt and freshly ground pepper
  to taste
1/4 cup thinly sliced green onions
1 1/2 teaspoons crushed garlic
1 1/2 cups sliced button
  mushrooms
1/3 cup brandy
1/2 cup beef bouillon
1/2 cup heavy cream
2 1/2 teaspoons Dijon mustard
1 tablespoon Worcestershire sauce
1/2 teaspoon hot red pepper sauce
1 tablespoon chopped
  fresh parsley

Steak Diane is believed to be an updated version of an ancient dish dedicated to the Roman goddess of the hunt, Diana. Originally, the recipe was used in cooking venison with a sauce that helped to tenderize the meat and add flavor.

RUBBED FLANK STEAK WITH HORSERADISH CREAM

Steak and Marinade

1/4 cup rye or bourbon whiskey

2 tablespoons low-sodium
soy sauce

1 (1 1/2-pound) flank steak

Horseradish Cream

1/3 cup plain fat-free yogurt

2 tablespoons
prepared horseradish

1 teaspoon Dijon mustard

1 large garlic clove, minced

Rub

1 tablespoon sugar

1 tablespoon paprika

1 tablespoon chili powder

1 1/2 teaspoons pepper

1 teaspoon garlic powder

1/8 teaspoon salt

For the steak and marinade, combine the whiskey and soy sauce in a large sealable plastic bag. Add the steak. Marinate in the refrigerator for 24 hours, turning the bag occasionally.

For the horseradish cream, combine the yogurt, horseradish, Dijon mustard and garlic in a small bowl and mix well. Cover and chill.

For the rub, combine the sugar, paprika, chili powder, pepper, garlic powder and salt in a small bowl and mix well. Rub the mixture into the steak. Chill for 30 minutes. Grill on an oiled rack over hot coals or broil for 9 to 10 minutes on each side or to the desired degree of doneness. Cut the steak diagonally across the grain into thin slices. Serve with the horseradish cream.

George Breckenridge generously donated the land of his private waterworks to San Antonio in 1899. Two years later, it was opened as Breckenridge Park and has since served as one of the city's main gathering places. San Antonio's first swimming pool was opened in 1915 at a bend in the river within the park.

MADEIRA SAUCE FOR BEEF

Use a skillet in which steaks have been sautéed or add some of the brown bits from a roasting pan.

Combine the water and flour in a small bowl and mix well. Heat the wine in the skillet, scraping up the brown bits. Stir in the flour mixture. Add the broth and pepper. Cook for 2 minutes, stirring constantly. Keep warm and serve with beef.

MAKES ABOUT 2 CUPS

1 cup water
2 tablespoons flour
1/2 cup madeira
1/2 cup beef broth
1/2 teaspoon freshly ground pepper

ROLLFLEISCH

Season the steaks with salt and pepper. Arrange the bacon on the steak slices. Roll up and secure with wooden picks. Sauté the steak rolls and onions in butter in a skillet until brown. Add the water and bouillon. Simmer, covered, for 1 hour or until tender.

Remove the steak rolls to a serving platter. Add 2 tablespoons flour for every 1 cup of liquid in the skillet, stirring until smooth. Add cream gradually, stirring constantly. Cook over medium heat until bubbly.

Remove the wooden picks. Serve the steak rolls with the gravy.

MAKES 8 SERVINGS

8 (1/4-inch-thick) slices
 round steak, tenderized
Salt and pepper to taste
8 to 10 slices bacon
Butter for sautéing
2 onions, chopped
2 cups water
1 beef bouillon cube
Flour
1/2 cup cream

The original German rouladen was created by rolling slices of beef around a mixture of pickle, bacon, and onion.

MAMA MIA MEATBALLS

Marinara Sauce
1 onion, finely chopped
3 to 4 tablespoons olive oil
2 or 3 garlic cloves, minced
3 pounds fresh tomatoes, peeled,
cored and crushed, or
48 ounces canned
crushed tomatoes
1 teaspoon dried oregano
Salt and pepper to taste
Crushed red pepper flakes to taste

Meatballs
1 to 1 1/2 pounds ground round
2 eggs, lightly beaten
3/4 cup bread crumbs
1/3 cup grated Parmesan cheese
1/4 teaspoon garlic powder
1/4 teaspoon onion powder
1/2 teaspoon salt
1/4 teaspoon pepper
1 teaspoon parsley flakes

For the sauce, sauté the onion in the olive oil in a large heavy skillet over medium heat for 4 to 5 minutes or until translucent. Add the garlic and increase the heat to medium-high. Add the tomatoes, oregano, salt and pepper. Cook for 15 minutes, stirring occasionally. Stir in red pepper flakes. Store in the refrigerator or freeze.

For the meatballs, combine the ground beef, eggs, bread crumbs, cheese, garlic powder, onion powder, salt, pepper and parsley flakes in a large bowl and mix well. Roll the mixture into 1- to 2-inch balls. Broil the meatballs in a broiler pan until slightly brown.

Combine the meatballs and sauce in a slow cooker. Cook on Low for at least 1 hour or up to 8 hours. The meatballs are best when cooked for a longer time.

MAKES 6 SERVINGS

BAKED STUFFED PUMPKIN

Cut the top off the pumpkin and set aside. Scoop out the seeds and membrane. Season the inside with salt and pepper. Rub the pumpkin inside and out with vegetable oil.

Brown the ground beef and sausage in a skillet, stirring until crumbly. Add the bell peppers and onion and cook until tender. Stir in the tomatoes with green chiles, tomato paste and brown sugar. Simmer for 20 minutes. Add the potatoes, corn, dill weed, Italian seasoning and cumin and mix well.

Spoon the mixture into the pumpkin and replace the top. Place the pumpkin on a baking sheet. Bake in a preheated 325-degree oven for 1 hour or until tender. Remove the top during the last 10 minutes of cooking so the liquid can reduce. Serve hot.

Taco seasoning mix may also be added. You may substitute rice for the potatoes.

MAKES 6 TO 8 SERVINGS

1 volleyball-size pumpkin
  (or three smaller pumpkins)
Salt and pepper to taste
Vegetable oil
1 1/2 pounds ground round
1 pound hot bulk pork sausage
1 large green bell pepper,
  chopped
1 large red bell pepper, chopped
1 large onion, chopped
1 (10-ounce) can tomatoes
  with green chiles
2 tablespoons tomato paste
2 tablespoons brown sugar
2 potatoes, diced and cooked
1 (8-ounce) package frozen
  whole kernel corn
2 teaspoons dried dill weed
2 teaspoons Italian seasoning
1 teaspoon cumin

BEEFY ENCHILADAS

1¹/2 pounds lean ground beef

1/2 cup chopped onion

2 teaspoons garlic powder

1¹/2 teaspoons salt

1 teaspoon pepper

8 cups beef broth

2 (14-ounce) cans peeled
whole tomatoes

3 tablespoons chili powder

4¹/2 teaspoons paprika

1 tablespoon ground cumin

1/3 cup cornstarch

1/3 cup water

Oil for frying

16 (6-inch) corn tortillas

6 cups (24 ounces) shredded
Cheddar cheese

1 cup chopped onions

Brown the ground beef and 1/2 cup onion in a skillet, stirring until the ground beef is crumbly; drain. Add the garlic powder, salt, pepper, broth, tomatoes, chili powder, paprika and cumin and mix well. Cook until the mixture comes to a boil, breaking up the tomatoes. Reduce the heat and simmer, uncovered, for 1 hour. Combine the cornstarch and water in a small bowl, stirring until smooth. Stir into the sauce gradually and cook for 5 minutes longer.

Heat 1/2 inch oil in a small skillet until hot but not smoking. Fry each tortilla for about 2 seconds on each side to soften. Combine the cheese and 1 cup onion in a medium bowl. Spoon 1/3 cup of the cheese mixture and a small amount of the beef sauce down the center of each tortilla. Roll up and place seam side down in two 11×17-inch baking dishes. Top with the remaining beef sauce. Bake in a preheated 350-degree oven for 10 to 12 minutes. Sprinkle with the remaining cheese mixture. Bake for 2 minutes longer or until the cheese melts.

MAKES 8 SERVINGS

Enchiladas are a traditional Mexican dish whose name literally means "seasoned with chiles." They are usually made with chicken, meat, or cheese stuffed into a tortilla. The traditional sauce is made with dried red chile peppers. Many people prefer a milder tomato-based red sauce, or a green sauce made with tomatillos and green chiles.

BOOT-SCOOTIN' CHILI

Brown the beef in the oil in a stockpot. Add water to cover. Add the bay leaves, chile powder, salt, garlic, cumin, oregano, cayenne pepper, black pepper, sugar, paprika and onion flakes and mix well. Simmer for 2 hours or until the beef is tender enough to shred. Remove the bay leaves. Chill overnight.

Combine the masa with a small amount of water, stirring until smooth. Add to the beef mixture and mix well. Add additional masa if you prefer a thicker chili or additional water if a thinner consistency is desired. Simmer until ready to serve, stirring occasionally and adding additional water to prevent burning.

Ladle into soup bowls and garnish with chopped onion, shredded sharp Cheddar cheese, sliced green onion tops and/or sour cream.

You may add 1 or 2 cans red chili beans if desired. Serve with crackers.

MAKES 8 SERVINGS

2$1/2$ to 3 pounds lean bottom
   round roast, cut into
   large cubes
3 tablespoons vegetable oil
2 bay leaves
6 tablespoons chile powder, or
   to taste
1 tablespoon salt
8 garlic cloves, minced
1 teaspoon cumin seeds or
   2 teaspoons ground cumin
1 teaspoon ground oregano
1 teaspoon cayenne pepper
1 teaspoon black pepper
1 teaspoon sugar
3 to 4 tablespoons Hungarian
   paprika
5 tablespoons dried onion flakes
5 or less tablespoons masa flour

For more than one hundred years, women dubbed "Chili Queens" appeared in the plazas of San Antonio at twilight to cook chili over open fires. People from all walks of life enjoyed chili and tamales under lantern light while being serenaded by mariachis.

ROSEMARY PORK TENDERLOINS WITH CAPER CREAM

Tenderloins

2 (1-pound) pork tenderloins
Prepared pesto
4 long stalks rosemary

Caper Cream

1/2 onion, chopped
1 tablespoon olive oil
1/2 cup white wine
2 tablespoons Dijon mustard
Coarse salt and freshly
ground pepper to taste
1/3 cup heavy cream
1 tablespoon capers,
roughly chopped

For the tenderloins, trim the tenderloins and cut halfway through lengthwise, folding back like a book. Spread pesto over the cut surface and close. Place one rosemary stalk on each side of the tenderloin and tie with kitchen twine. Grill until a meat thermometer inserted in the thickest portion reads 160 degrees.

For the caper cream, sauté the onion in the olive oil in a saucepan until tender. Add the wine and Dijon mustard and mix well. Cook until slightly reduced. Season with salt and pepper and cook until further reduced. Add the cream and capers. Reduce the heat.

To serve, slice the tenderloin into medallions and top with the caper cream.

MAKES 4 SERVINGS

Located in downtown San Antonio, the Alamo is a partially reconstructed Spanish mission and museum. In 1836, a battle to defend the Alamo against the powerful Mexican army was lost, but it is credited with sparking the successful fight for Texan independence. The Alamo and nearby Riverwalk are the top two tourist attractions in Texas.

PORK TENDERLOIN WITH TABASCO ONIONS

Combine the tenderloin and Worcestershire sauce to taste in a sealable plastic bag, turning to coat. Marinate at room temperature for 15 to 30 minutes.

Melt the butter in a large skillet over medium-high heat. Add the onions, 3 dashes Worcestershire sauce and Tabasco sauce. Cook for 10 to 15 minutes or until the onions are brown, stirring occasionally. Reduce the heat if the onions seem to be browning too quickly. Reduce the heat to medium-low and add the sugar. Cook, covered, for 15 minutes.

Drain the tenderloin, reserving the marinade. Heat a small amount of olive oil in an ovenproof skillet. Add the tenderloin and sear on all sides for 1 minute or until brown. Pour the reserved marinade over the tenderloin. Roast in a preheated 425-degree oven for 10 minutes or until a meat thermometer inserted in the thickest portion reads 155 to 160 degrees. Tent with foil and let stand for 10 minutes. Slice into medallions and serve over the onions. Top with the cheese.

MAKES 4 TO 6 SERVINGS

2 pounds pork tenderloin
Worcestershire sauce to taste
2 tablespoons butter
3 large white onions,
   cut into slices
3 dashes Worcestershire sauce
10 dashes Tabasco sauce, or
   to taste
1 teaspoon sugar
Olive oil
1/4 cup crumbled feta cheese

When soaking meat in a marinade, make certain the marinade is cold and the meat is completely covered. The longer the meat is left to marinate, the more pungent its taste will be.

LAMB SHANKS A LA HELEN

6 lamb shanks
1/2 lemon
1/2 teaspoon garlic powder
11/2 cups flour
1 tablespoon salt
3/4 teaspoon pepper
3/4 cup vegetable oil
2 (10-ounce) cans condensed
beef consommé
2 cups water
3/4 cup dry vermouth
2 onions, chopped
6 carrots, peeled and
cut into chunks
6 ribs celery, cut into chunks

Rub the lamb shanks with lemon and sprinkle with the garlic powder. Let stand for 15 minutes. Combine the flour, salt and pepper in a sealable plastic bag. Add the lamb shanks one at a time, shaking to coat. Reserve the remaining flour. Brown the lamb shanks in the hot oil in a large skillet. Arrange in a baking dish in one layer. Add 6 tablespoons of the reserved flour to the pan drippings. Cook until the flour browns, whisking constantly. Add the consommé, water, and vermouth and mix well. Cook until slightly thickened, and then add the onions. Pour the mixture over the lamb shanks. Bake, uncovered, in a preheated 350-degree oven for 1 to 2 hours. Turn the lamb shanks and add the carrots and celery. Bake for 1 hour longer or until the lamb shanks are very tender.

MAKES 6 SERVINGS

BARBECUED LAMB CHOPS

1/3 cup firmly packed brown sugar
1/4 cup soy sauce
2 tablespoons ketchup
1 tablespoon lemon juice
1/2 teaspoon ground ginger
1/4 teaspoon salt
1/4 teaspoon pepper
1/8 teaspoon garlic powder
4 (1-inch-thick) lamb chops

Combine the brown sugar, soy sauce, ketchup, lemon juice, ginger, salt, pepper and garlic powder in a bowl and mix well. Grill the lamb chops for 7 minutes on each side until medium-rare (slightly pink inside), basting often with the sauce.

MAKES 4 SERVINGS

CHERRY- AND PISTACHIO-STUFFED CHICKEN

Mix the red wine, sugar and 1/2 cup of the dried cherries in a bowl. Let stand for 1 hour. Add the pistachios. Cut a slit in each chicken breast, forming a pocket. Fill each pocket with the cherry mixture. Brown the chicken on each side in the hot oil in a skillet for 5 minutes. Season with salt and pepper. Place in a baking dish. Bake in a preheated 425-degree oven for 10 to 20 minutes or until cooked through. Add the butter and shallot to the skillet and cook for 3 minutes. Add the port and white wine and cook until reduced to about 1/4 cup. Whisk in the Dijon mustard, vinegar and preserves. Add the remaining 1/2 cup dried cherries and season with salt and pepper. Drizzle over the chicken.

MAKES 8 SERVINGS

1/2 cup red wine or port
1/4 cup sugar
1 cup dried cherries
1/4 cup pistachios
8 chicken breasts
2 tablespoons vegetable oil
Salt and pepper to taste
2 tablespoons butter
1 shallot, minced
1/4 to 1/2 cup port
1/4 to 1/2 cup white wine
1 tablespoon Dijon mustard
1 tablespoon cherry vinegar
2 tablespoons cherry preserves

ORANGE CHICKEN

Combine the orange juice, sugar, cornstarch, cinnamon and ginger in a saucepan and mix well. Cook over medium heat until thickened, stirring constantly. Stir in the pecans. Remove from the heat. Brown the chicken in hot oil in a skillet. Stir in the water, paprika, salt and pepper. Bring to a boil and reduce the heat to low. Simmer, covered, for 35 minutes, turning once. Serve the chicken with the sauce and garnish with orange slices. You may substitute pork chops for chicken breasts.

MAKES 6 SERVINGS

1 cup orange juice
1/2 cup sugar
1 tablespoon cornstarch
1/2 teaspoon cinnamon
1/4 teaspoon ground ginger
3/4 cup chopped pecans
6 chicken breasts
3/4 cup water
1/2 teaspoon paprika
Salt to taste
1/4 teaspoon pepper

131

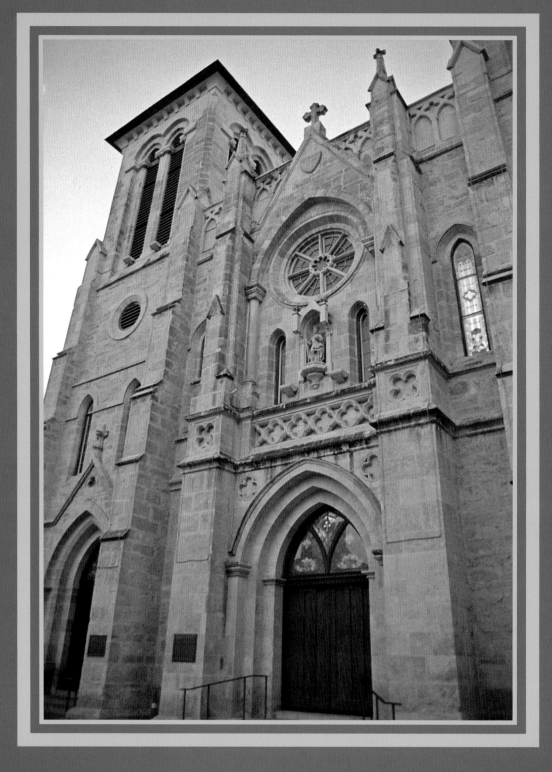

SAN FERNANDO CATHEDRAL

*In 1730, Canary Island settlers founded Villa San Fernando de Bexar for Spain.
It was the first permanent settlement in Texas. Built at the original church site,
San Fernando Cathedral sits in the heart of downtown San Antonio. Still serving as
an active religious center, it has the oldest cathedral sanctuary in the United States.*

CHICKEN ROLLS

Pound the chicken to a 1/4-inch thickness. Combine the butter and garlic in a shallow dish. Combine the croutons, cheese, parsley, salt, pepper and paprika in another shallow dish. Brush each side of the chicken with the butter mixture. Coat in the crouton mixture. Roll up and secure with a wooden pick. Place seam side down in a lightly greased baking dish. Sprinkle lemon juice over each chicken roll. Bake in a preheated 350-degree oven for 35 to 45 minutes or until cooked through. Serve whole or cut into slices.

MAKES 8 SERVINGS

8 boneless skinless chicken breasts
1/2 cup (1 stick) butter, melted
1 garlic clove, chopped
1 1/2 cups toasted dry croutons, finely crushed
2/3 cup finely grated Parmesan cheese
1 1/2 teaspoons chopped fresh parsley
Salt and pepper to taste
1 teaspoon paprika
Juice of 1 lemon

LIGHT CHICKEN CORDON BLEU

Slice each chicken breast horizontally from the thinner side to, but not through, the opposite side. Spread each chicken breast open and arrange one-fourth of the ham and cheese on each. Close the chicken over the filling. Beat the egg whites, Dijon mustard and buttermilk in a bowl until smooth. Combine the bread crumbs, cheese and pepper in a shallow dish and mix well. Carefully dip the chicken into the crumb mixture, then the egg mixture, and the crumb mixture again. Arrange on a greased rack on a baking sheet. Bake in a preheated 400-degree oven for 30 to 35 minutes or until golden brown and cooked through.

MAKES 4 SERVINGS

4 boneless skinless chicken breasts
2 ounces ham, thinly sliced and cut into 1/2-inch strips
2 ounces Gruyère cheese, thinly sliced and cut into 1/2-inch strips
2 egg whites
1 tablespoon Dijon mustard
1/4 cup buttermilk
2/3 cup fine dry bread crumbs
1/4 cup (1 ounce) Parmesan cheese
Freshly ground pepper to taste

133

CHICKEN TAQUITOS WITH POBLANO PEPPERS

4 cups water

1 teaspoon salt

1 onion, cut into halves

2 garlic cloves

2 large chicken breasts

2 roasted poblano chiles, seeded and sliced

18 corn tortillas

3 large ripe tomatoes

1/2 cup water

1 teaspoon chicken bouillon granules

1 tablespoon olive oil

Salt and pepper to taste

16 ounces white Cheddar cheese, shredded

Bring 4 cups water to a boil in a saucepan. Add 1 teaspoon salt, half the onion, the garlic and chicken and boil for 30 minutes; cool. (Add some carrots and zucchini to the mixture for chicken soup.) Remove the chicken and shred. Arrange a small amount of the chicken and a poblano chile slice in each tortilla. Fold the tortilla over to enclose the filling. Arrange in a greased 9×13-inch baking dish.

Process the tomatoes, 1/2 cup water, the bouillon granules and remaining onion half in a blender or food processor until puréed. Combine the olive oil and tomato mixture in a saucepan and mix well. Cook for 20 minutes or until the mixture boils. Season with salt and pepper to taste. Pour over the tortillas. Top with the cheese. Bake in a preheated 350-degree oven for 30 minutes. Serve with shredded lettuce and avocado slices.

MAKES 4 SERVINGS

Roasting peppers loosens their skins and enhances their natural sweetness. To roast poblano peppers, cut them lengthwise into halves. Remove the ribs and seeds. Place the pepper skin side up on a baking sheet or broiler pan, or skin side down on a grill over high heat. Roast until the skin blisters and is light brown. Place the peppers in a paper bag for 10 minutes to steam. Skins should slip off easily.

PAPRIKA CHICKEN BAKE

Arrange the chicken in a single layer in a large baking pan. Combine the oil, liquid smoke, Nature's Seasoning and garlic powder in a small bowl and mix well. Pour over the chicken. Sprinkle generously with paprika. Cover tightly with foil. Bake in a preheated 325-degree oven for 1 1/2 hours.

MAKES 6 TO 8 SERVINGS

6 to 8 boneless chicken breasts, or 1 chicken, cut up
1/4 cup vegetable oil
1 tablespoon liquid smoke
1 teaspoon Nature's Seasons Seasoning Blend
1/2 teaspoon garlic powder
Paprika

CHICKEN JAMBALAYA

Sauté the onion, bell pepper, celery, oregano and thyme in the oil in a large skillet. Add the sausage and cook for several minutes. Stir in the chicken, rice and garlic. Cook for 3 minutes. Add the remaining ingredients and bring to a boil. Reduce the heat and simmer, covered, for 20 to 25 minutes or until the rice is tender.

MAKES 6 TO 8 SERVINGS

Jambalaya is a versatile Cajun-Creole dish whose name originates from the Spanish word for ham, which was the primary meat used in the first jambalayas. Today there are countless variations of this meat, rice, and vegetable dish.

1 onion, chopped
1/2 cup chopped green bell pepper
2 tablespoons chopped celery
1 1/2 teaspoons dried oregano
1/4 teaspoon thyme
2 tablespoons vegetable oil
8 ounces smoked sausage, sliced
2 cups chopped uncooked chicken
2 cups rice
2 garlic cloves, minced
2 teaspoons Louisiana hot sauce
1 bay leaf
1 (28-ounce) can chopped tomatoes
1/4 cup tomato paste
2 to 4 cups chicken broth
Freshly ground pepper to taste

135

DOVES AU VIN

1 cup all-purpose flour
1 teaspoon salt
1 teaspoon pepper
12 doves, dressed
1/3 cup butter
1 cup chopped celery
1 cup chopped onion
1 small green bell pepper, chopped
1 (10-ounce) can beef broth
1/2 cup dry red wine
Hot cooked noodles or rice

Combine the flour, salt and pepper in a large sealable plastic bag, shaking to blend. Add the doves a few at a time and shake to coat. Melt the butter in a large nonstick skillet over medium-high heat. Add the doves and cook until brown, turning once. Place the doves in a lightly greased 9×13-inch baking dish. Sprinkle with the celery, onion and bell pepper. Add the broth. Bake, covered with foil, in a preheated 350-degree oven for 1 1/2 hours. Pour the wine over the doves and bake, covered, for 30 minutes longer. Serve over noodles.

MAKES 6 SERVINGS

QUAIL ON A STICK

15 quail breasts, deboned
1 1/2 cups teriyaki sauce
1/2 cup water
Freshly ground pepper, garlic salt
and onion salt to taste
1 bottle barbecue sauce

Combine the quail, teriyaki sauce and water in a dish. Marinate for 30 minutes. Soak wooden skewers in water for 30 minutes. Arrange about four quail pieces on each skewer. Sprinkle with pepper, garlic salt and onion salt. Cook in a skillet or on a grill over low heat for about 15 minutes, turning frequently. Baste with the barbecue sauce. Cook for 5 minutes longer.

MAKES 6 TO 8 SERVINGS

Birds such as dove, quail, and pheasant should be cooked until firm but still juicy. If the meat is dry and tough, it has probably been overcooked.

SOUTHWEST SALMON TOSTADA

Cut the tomatoes into halves. Combine with the cilantro, onion, garlic, olive oil, salt and pepper in a large bowl and mix well. Grill the salmon in one piece until cooked through. Cut the fillet into four pieces and slide a spatula under each piece to remove the skin. Place a salmon piece on each tostado shell. Top with equal amounts of the black beans, tomato mixture, sour cream and avocado slices. Top each with one tortilla chip. For a spicier tomato mixture, add a small amount of minced jalapeño chile and lime juice.

MAKES 4 SERVINGS

1 pint red grape tomatoes

1 pint yellow grape tomatoes

1 tablespoon chopped cilantro

1/2 cup chopped white onion

1 or 2 garlic cloves, minced

1 tablespoon olive oil

Salt and pepper to taste

1 (1-pound) salmon fillet, skin on

1 (15-ounce) can black
    beans, heated

1/4 cup sour cream (optional)

2 ripe avocados, sliced

4 tostado shells

4 tortilla chips

GINGER SALMON FILLETS

Combine the soy sauce, olive oil, white wine, garlic, sesame oil and ginger in a bowl. Arrange the vegetables and mushrooms in a 9×13-inch baking dish. Place the salmon on top of the vegetables. Sprinkle with the green onions. Pour the soy sauce mixture over the salmon. Bake, covered with foil, in a preheated 425-degree oven for 20 minutes or until cooked through. Remove foil and broil until brown and glazed, if desired. May use squash, zucchini, broccoli, and/or bok choy as the chopped vegetables.

MAKES 4 SERVINGS

1/3 cup soy sauce

2 tablespoons olive oil

2 tablespoons white wine

2 garlic cloves, minced

1 tablespoon plus 2 teaspoons
    sesame oil

1 (2-inch) piece fresh ginger,
    chopped

2 cups chopped vegetables

8 ounces mushrooms, sliced

11/2 pounds salmon fillets

2 green onions, sliced

137

TILAPIA FLORENTINE

8 ounces fresh mushrooms, sliced
1 small onion, chopped
1 teaspoon olive oil
8 ounces fresh baby spinach
4 tilapia fillets
Garlic powder and salt to taste
2 teaspoons sherry
1 cup (4 ounces) shredded
mozzarella cheese

Sauté the mushrooms and onion in the hot olive oil in a large skillet until tender. Add the spinach. Stir-fry until wilted. Remove from the heat. Arrange half the spinach mixture in a greased 8×10-inch baking dish. Top with the fillets and sprinkle with garlic powder and salt. Top with the remaining spinach mixture. Sprinkle with the sherry and cheese. Bake in a preheated 400-degree oven for 15 to 20 minutes or until the cheese is light brown and the fish flakes easily.

MAKES 2 TO 4 SERVINGS

TILAPIA AMANDINE

2 tablespoons sliced almonds
1 tablespoon butter
2 teaspoons vegetable oil
1/4 cup all-purpose flour
Salt and pepper to taste
2 tilapia fillets (or other delicate
white fish fillets)
1/4 cup white wine
1 tablespoon plus
1 teaspoon lemon juice
2 tablespoons butter
1 garlic clove, minced (optional)
1/4 cup chopped fresh parsley

Toast the almonds in a skillet for 4 to 5 minutes or until brown.

Heat 1 tablespoon butter and the oil in a large skillet. Combine the flour, salt and pepper in a sealable plastic bag. Add the fillets and shake to coat. Cook the fillets in the hot butter mixture for 4 minutes on each side or until golden brown. Remove to a serving platter. Add the wine, lemon juice, 2 tablespoons butter and the garlic to the skillet. Pour the mixture over the fish. Top with the toasted almonds and parsley.

MAKES 2 SERVINGS

"In the hands of an able cook, fish can become an inexhaustible source of perpetual delight."
—*Jean Anthelme Brilliat-Savarin*

SHRIMP AND ASPARAGUS IN PUFF PASTRY

Sauté the mushrooms and onion in the butter and wine in a skillet until the liquid has evaporated. Season with pepper and mix with the shrimp and asparagus in a bowl. Spoon into six 8-ounce ovenproof ramekins or a greased baking dish. Top each evenly with the cream cheese. Cut the puff pastry to fit 1/4 inch larger than the top of each ramekin. Moisten the rim of each and top with the pastry. Crimp to seal and press onto the rim. Combine the egg yolk and milk. Brush over the top of the pastry. Cut several steam vents. Bake in a preheated 425-degree oven for 12 to 15 minutes or until light brown.

MAKES 6 SERVINGS

2 cups finely chopped mushrooms
2 tablespoons minced onion
1 tablespoon butter
1 tablespoon white wine
Pepper to taste
12 ounces cooked shrimp
1 pound fresh asparagus, trimmed
*   and cut into 1/2-inch pieces*
8 ounces cream cheese, softened
*   and cut into cubes*
4 sheets puff pastry
1 egg yolk
2 tablespoons milk

FIVE-SPICE SCALLOPS

Sauté the green onions, garlic and red pepper flakes in the hot oil in a skillet over medium heat for 1 minute. Add the next four ingredients. Cook for 3 to 5 minutes or until the scallops are just cooked through; do not overcook. Remove with a slotted spoon to a plate. Add the lemon juice and butter to the skillet. Cook for 1 minute or until the mixture thickens. Add any scallop juices that have gathered on the plate. Cook briefly to thicken. Remove the skillet from the heat and add the scallops. Cook until heated through, stirring constantly. Top with the parsley and serve.

MAKES 2 SERVINGS

2 small green onions, thinly sliced
1 garlic clove, minced
Pinch of red pepper flakes
2 teaspoons vegetable oil
10 to 12 ounces scallops
1/2 teaspoon five-spice powder
1/4 teaspoon salt
Freshly ground black pepper to taste
2 tablespoons lemon juice
1 teaspoon butter or margarine
1 tablespoon minced fresh parsley
*   (optional)*

This pretty fountain at the Garden Center of San Antonio Botanical Garden is the site of Assistance League® of San Antonio monthly meetings and annual Valentine Tea.

DELICIOUS DESSERTS

NOW SERVING: SWEET SMILES

When you serve a favorite dessert to your family or friends, you know that the greatest reward you can receive is a smile that expresses their joy and gratitude. They appreciate that you made an effort to provide them with a special treat.

Volunteers seek to accomplish the same effect when they create unique designs on baseball caps. Utilizing many different concepts, from fairy tale and comic book characters to seasonal and holiday symbols, mammals and fish, and encouraging words and phrases, the **CAPS** (Caps Art Promotes Smiles) project seeks to put smiles on the faces of acutely or chronically ill children, from toddlers to teens. When the young recipients get to personally select a hand-decorated cap, their surprise and happiness is reflected in their joyous smiles.

COUNTRY HARVEST	FAMILY AND FRIENDS FALL SUPPER
Blue Cheese-Stuffed Mushrooms page 14	
Cream of Pecan Soup with	*Artichoke Spread with*
Chipotle Cream page 56	*Toasted Baguette Slices* page 21
Rosemary Pork Tenderloins with	*Apple Spinach Salad* page 61
Caper Cream page 128	*Rollfleisch* page 123
Gourmet Wild Rice page 114	*Chicken Rolls* page 133
Spiced Peaches page 107	*Day-Ahead Mashed Potatoes* page 101
Apple Cake with Rum Sauce page 151	*South-of-Border Green Beans* page 100
Merlot or Zinfandel	*Chocolate Almond Torte with*
	Chocolate Sauce page 150
	Cabernet Sauvignon

PRALINE-CRUSTED CHEESECAKE

2 cups crushed shortbread cookies

3 tablespoons butter, melted

4 praline candies, coarsely crumbled

40 ounces cream cheese, softened

1³/4 cups sugar

2 tablespoons all-purpose flour

1¹/2 teaspoons vanilla extract

4 eggs

2 egg yolks

¹/3 cup whipping cream

1 teaspoon grated lemon zest

2 cups sour cream

¹/3 cup sugar

Combine the crushed cookies and butter in a large bowl and mix well. Press over the bottom and up the side of a greased 10-inch springform pan. Bake in a preheated 350-degree oven for 8 minutes. Cool on a wire rack. Sprinkle the pralines over the crust.

Beat the cream cheese in a large bowl with an electric mixer set at medium speed until creamy. Beat in 1³/4 cups sugar, the flour and vanilla gradually. Beat in the eggs and egg yolks one at a time, beating just until the yellow disappears. Stir in the whipping cream and lemon zest. Pour into the prepared crust. Place the pan on a foil-lined baking sheet. Bake in a preheated 350-degree oven on the lower rack of the oven for 10 minutes. Reduce the oven temperature to 325 degrees. Bake for 1 hour and 20 minutes longer or until almost set. Cool on a wire rack for 1 hour.

Combine the sour cream and ¹/3 cup sugar in a bowl and mix well. Spread over the cheesecake. Bake in a preheated 325-degree oven for 10 minutes. Cool on a wire rack. Chill, covered, for 8 hours. Remove the side of pan. Garnish with crumbled pralines.

MAKES 12 SERVINGS

Springform pans are most often used for delicate desserts that can't be turned upside-down. Their removable sides make them practical for any dish that needs to be removed from its pan for serving. They come in a variety of sizes and shapes.

MUD PIE

For the pie, combine the cookie crumbs and butter in a large bowl and mix well. Press over the bottom and up the side of a greased 9-inch springform pan. Chill until firm.

Spoon half the ice cream into the crust. Freeze untiil firm. Combine the chocolate chips, marshmallows and evaporated milk in a medium saucepan and cook until melted and thickened, stirring constantly. Stir in the vanilla. Remove from the heat and cool. Pour half the sauce over the frozen ice cream. Add the remaining softened ice cream. Top with the remaining sauce.

For the topping, whip the cream with the liqueur and confectioners' sugar in a bowl until firm peaks form. Spoon over the pie, spreading evenly. Sprinkle with the pecans. Garnish with chocolate curls. Serve or store in the freezer.

MAKES 8 TO 10 SERVINGS

San Antonians use any excuse to celebrate, including the annual draining, cleaning, and refilling of the San Antonio River. There is even a coronation of a "Mud King and Queen."

Pie
24 chocolate sandwich cookies, crushed
1/4 cup (1/2 stick) butter, melted
1/2 gallon rich coffee ice cream, softened
2 cups (12 ounces) semisweet chocolate chips
2 cups miniature marshmallows
2 cups evaporated milk
2 tablespoons vanilla extract

Topping
1 cup heavy whipping cream
1/4 cup Kahlúa
1/4 cup confectioners' sugar
1/2 cup chopped pecans, walnuts or hazelnuts

PECAN CARAMEL CHOCOLATE MOUSSE PIE

Pastry
1/2 cup shortening
1 cup all-purpose flour
Dash of salt
1/4 cup ice water

Filling
1/2 cup (1 stick) butter, melted
1 cup sugar
4 eggs
1 cup light corn syrup
Dash of salt
1 tablespoon rum
2 cups chopped lightly toasted pecans

Topping
1 cup sugar
1/2 cup baking cocoa
2 cups heavy whipping cream
1/2 cup butterscotch caramel topping
1/2 cup milk chocolate topping

For the pastry, cut the shortening into the flour in a bowl using a pastry blender or two knives until the mixture resembles coarse crumbs. Sprinkle with salt and ice water. Blend until the mixture forms a ball; do not overmix. Roll out to a 1/8-inch thickness on a floured surface. Fit into a 10-inch pie plate. Trim the edge.

For the filling, combine the butter, sugar, eggs, corn syrup, salt, rum and pecans in the order listed in a bowl and mix well. Spoon into the prepared pie shell. Bake in a preheated 450-degree oven for 15 minutes. Reduce the heat to 350 degrees and bake for 30 to 40 minutes longer or until set. Cool and chill in the refrigerator.

For the topping, combine the sugar and baking cocoa in a mixing bowl. Add the cream and beat at high speed until stiff peaks form.

Spread half the butterscotch caramel topping over the filling. Spoon the cream topping over the butterscotch caramel topping, spreading to the edge. Drizzle with the remaining butterscotch caramel topping in a checkerboard pattern. Rotate the pie a quarter-turn and drizzle with the milk chocolate topping in the same manner. Garnish with pecan halves. Chill until serving time.

MAKES 10 SERVINGS

HEAVENLY ANGEL LEMON PIE

Beat the egg whites in a bowl until foamy. Add the salt and cream of tartar. Beat until stiff peaks form, adding 1 cup sugar gradually. Spread the meringue in a buttered 9-inch pie plate, smoothing the mixture into a crust shape. Bake in a preheated 275-degree oven for 25 minutes. The meringue will puff up during baking, then settle and crack as it cools. Beat the egg yolks in a small saucepan. Stir in 3/4 cup sugar, the lemon juice and zest. Cook over low heat until thickened, stirring constantly. Cool for 1 hour or until completely cool. The mixture will continue to thicken during cooling. Beat 1 1/2 cups of the cream in a bowl until thickened. Fold into the cooled lemon filling. Spoon into the meringue shell. Beat the remaining 1/2 cup cream in a bowl, adding sugar to taste gradually. Stir in vanilla. Spread over the filling. Refrigerate for several hours or overnight.

4 egg whites
Pinch of salt
1/4 teaspoon cream of tartar
1 cup sugar
6 egg yolks
3/4 cup sugar
1/3 cup plus 1 tablespoon fresh lemon juice
Grated zest of 2 lemons
2 cups heavy whipping cream
Sugar to taste
Vanilla extract to taste (optional)

MAKES 8 SERVINGS

MARGARITA PIE

Combine the sweetened condensed milk, lime juice, tequila and Triple Sec in a bowl and mix well. Fold in the whipped topping. Pour into the pie shell. Freeze for 4 hours or until firm.

1 (14-ounce) can sweetened condensed milk
1/3 cup lime juice
1/4 cup (or more) tequila
2 tablespoons (or more) Triple Sec
1 cup whipped topping
1 baked shortbread pie crust

MAKES 8 SERVINGS

145

COLONIAL CHESS PECAN PIE

1/2 cup (1 stick) butter, softened
1 cup sugar
1 tablespoon all-purpose flour
1/8 teaspoon salt
3 egg yolks
1/2 cup evaporated milk
1 teaspoon vanilla extract
1 unbaked deep-dish pie shell
2/3 cup coarsely chopped pecans

Beat the butter and sugar in a bowl until fluffy. Beat in the flour, salt and egg yolks. Stir in the evaporated milk and vanilla. Pour into the pie shell. Sprinkle with the pecans. Bake in a preheated 425-degree oven for 10 minutes. Reduce the heat to 325 degrees and bake for 40 minutes longer.

MAKES 6 TO 8 SERVINGS

LEMON CHESS PIE

2 cups sugar
1 tablespoon all-purpose flour
1 tablespoon cornmeal
4 eggs
1/4 cup (1/2 stick) butter, melted
1/4 cup milk
Juice of 1 lemon
Grated lemon zest to taste
1 unbaked (9-inch) pie shell

Mix the sugar, flour and cornmeal in a medium bowl. Add the eggs, butter, milk, lemon juice and lemon zest. Beat until smooth and blended. Pour into the pie shell. Bake in a preheated 350-degree oven for 45 minutes or until set.

MAKES 8 SERVINGS

Lemon zest is the flavorful yellow outer layer of a lemon's skin. Avoid the bitter white layer of pith just under the zest.

PINEAPPLE BREAD PUDDING WITH COCONUT SAUCE

Beat the cream cheese, brown sugar, eggs, milk and vanilla in a mixing bowl until smooth. Stir in the pineapple and coconut. Fold in the bread cubes. Pour into a greased 1¹/2-quart baking dish. Bake in a preheated 375-degree oven for 30 minutes or until the center is set or a knife inserted in the center comes out clean. Combine the sour cream and cream of coconut in a bowl and mix well. Serve with the pudding.

MAKES 6 TO 8 SERVINGS

8 ounces cream cheese, softened
1 cup packed light brown sugar
6 eggs
1 cup milk
1 teaspoon vanilla extract
1 can crushed pineapple, drained
2 cups flaked coconut
8 slices sandwich bread, trimmed,
*   cubed and lightly toasted*
1 cup sour cream
1 cup cream of coconut

COLD LEMON CHARLOTTE

Mix the zest, egg yolks and 1¹/2 cups sugar in the top of a double boiler over simmering water. Cook for 15 minutes, stirring occasionally. Combine the juice and gelatin in a small saucepan over low heat, stirring to dissolve; cool. Stir into the egg mixture. Beat the whipping cream in a bowl until stiff peaks form. Fold the egg whites and whipped cream into the lemon mixture. Line the bottom and side of a 9-inch springform pan with ladyfingers. Spoon in half the lemon filling. Top with the remaining ladyfingers and lemon mixture. Chill for 3 hours or until set. Remove from the pan. Add sugar to taste to the raspberry purée. Serve with the charlotte.

MAKES 12 SERVINGS

Grated zest of 3 lemons
6 egg yolks
1¹/2 cups sugar
Juice of 3 lemons
2 envelopes unflavored gelatin
2 cups heavy whipping cream
6 egg whites, stiffly beaten
3 packages ladyfingers,
*   split lengthwise*
Sugar to taste
1 (10- to 12-ounce) package
*   frozen raspberries, puréed*
*   and strained*

147

CREME CARAMEL (FLAN)

1 cup milk

1 cup light cream

1 vanilla bean, or

1/2 to 1 teaspoon
vanilla extract

1/4 cup sugar

3 eggs

1 egg yolk

1/2 teaspoon vanilla extract

1 cup sugar

6 tablespoons water

Preheat the oven to 350 degrees.

Combine the milk, cream, vanilla bean and 1/4 cup sugar in a saucepan and bring to a boil. Remove from the heat. Let steep, covered, for 5 to 10 minutes.

Combine the eggs and egg yolk in a bowl and beat lightly. Remove the vanilla bean. Stir the milk mixture into the beaten eggs. Stir in 1/2 teaspoon vanilla and set aside.

Combine 1 cup sugar and the water in a 4-cup ovenproof ring mold. Swirl the pan over low heat until the sugar dissolves. Increase the heat and boil rapidly without stirring until the syrup becomes a rich, dark caramel. To prevent the syrup from burning in the hot mold, remove from the heat before the syrup is quite ready. Using oven gloves or kitchen towels, swirl the mold to coat evenly with the caramel. Cool slightly.

Pour the egg mixture into the prepared mold. Cover with foil and place in a baking pan. Pour enough hot water into the baking pan to reach halfway up the side of the ring mold.

Place the baking pan in the oven and reduce the temperature to 325 degrees. Bake for 35 to 40 minutes or until set; cool. Invert the mold onto a plate or serving dish that will catch the caramel syrup. Garnish with fresh fruit such as grapes, strawberries, raspberries or cherries.

MAKES 4 TO 6 SERVINGS

Flan is a popular dessert favored by both the Spanish and Mexicans. If you like to experiment with flavors, try substituting coconut, pistachio, almond, or lemon flavors for the usual vanilla flavoring.

FESTIVE CRANBERRY TORTE

For the crust, combine the graham cracker crumbs, pecans, sugar and butter in a bowl and mix well. Press over the bottom and up the side of an 8- to 10-inch springform pan; chill.

For the filling, combine the cranberries and sugar in a mixing bowl and let stand for 5 minutes. Add the egg whites, orange juice concentrate, vanilla and salt and beat at high speed for 6 to 8 minutes or until soft peaks form.

Beat the cream in a mixing bowl until soft peaks form. Fold into the cranberry mixture. Spoon into the prepared crust. Freeze until firm.

For the glaze, combine the sugar and cornstarch in a saucepan. Add the cranberries and water and mix well. Cook until bubbly, stirring constantly. Cook until the cranberries pop, stirring constantly. Cool to room temperature.

To serve, loosen and remove the side of the pan and place the torte on a serving platter. Spoon the cranberry glaze over the center of the torte. Arrange orange slices around the torte.

MAKES 8 TO 10 SERVINGS

Crust

1 1/2 cups graham cracker crumbs
1/2 cup chopped pecans
1/4 cup sugar
6 tablespoons butter, melted

Filling

2 cups whole fresh cranberries, lightly ground
1 cup sugar
2 egg whites
1 tablespoon frozen orange juice concentrate, thawed
1 teaspoon vanilla extract
1/8 teaspoon salt
1 cup heavy whipping cream

Cranberry Glaze

1/2 cup sugar
1 tablespoon cornstarch
3/4 cup fresh cranberries
2/3 cup water

To Serve

Orange slices, cut into quarters

Cranberries, blueberries, and Concord grapes are the only fruits native to the United States. Fresh cranberries are available from September through December.

149

CHOCOLATE ALMOND TORTE WITH CHOCOLATE SAUCE

Torte

8 ounces bittersweet or semisweet
chocolate, chopped
2 1/4 cups sliced almonds, toasted
(about 8 ounces)
1 cup granulated sugar
6 egg yolks
1/2 teaspoon vanilla extract
6 egg whites
1/8 teaspoon cream of tartar
Confectioners' sugar
Chocolate curls (optional)

Chocolate Sauce

3/4 cup sugar
1/2 cup baking cocoa
1 (5-ounce) can evaporated milk
1/3 cup light corn syrup
1/3 cup butter or margarine
1 teaspoon vanilla extract

For the torte, combine the chocolate, almonds and granulated sugar in a food processor. Process until the mixture is finely chopped and grainy. Beat the egg yolks and vanilla in a large bowl until pale yellow and thick. Fold in the chocolate mixture. (The mixture will be quite thick.) Beat the egg whites in another large bowl with clean beaters until foamy. Add the cream of tartar and beat until stiff peaks form. Fold into the batter one-third at a time. Pour into a buttered 9-inch springform pan. Bake in a preheated 350-degree oven for 45 minutes or until the top is golden brown and a tester inserted into the center comes out clean. Remove to a wire rack to cool. Run a knife around the side of the pan to loosen. Remove the side of the pan and place the torte on a serving platter. Sift confectioners' sugar over the torte and top with chocolate curls.

For the chocolate sauce, combine the sugar and baking cocoa in a saucepan. Stir in the evaporated milk and corn syrup. Bring to a boil over medium heat, stirring constantly. Boil for 1 minute, stirring constantly. Remove from the heat and stir in the butter and vanilla. Store any leftovers in the refrigerator. Drizzle some of the warm chocolate sauce on each serving plate and top with a slice of the torte. Serve with ice cream.

MAKES 8 SERVINGS

Before beating egg whites, let them stand at room temperature for twenty to thirty minutes. Warmer whites produce a greater volume when beaten.

APPLE CAKE WITH RUM SAUCE

For the cake, beat the shortening and sugar in a large bowl. Beat in the salt, egg, cinnamon, nutmeg, baking soda, flour, hot water and vanilla. Stir in the nuts and apples.

Spoon the batter into a greased 9-inch cake pan or pie plate. Bake in a preheated 350-degree oven for 45 minutes to 1 hour or until the cake tests done. The cake can be frozen. Thaw and reheat before serving.

For the sauce, melt the butter in a small saucepan. Stir in the brown sugar. Bring the mixture to a boil and boil for 2 minutes. Add the cream and boil for several seconds. Remove from the heat and stir in the rum extract.

To serve, spoon some of the rum sauce over the warm cake.

MAKES 6 TO 8 SERVINGS

Cake

1/4 cup shortening

1 cup sugar

1/4 teaspoon salt

1 egg

1 teaspoon cinnamon

1 teaspon nutmeg

1 teaspoon baking soda

1 cup all-purpose flour

2 tablespoons hot water

1 teaspoon vanilla extract

1/2 cup nuts, chopped

2 1/2 cups chopped peeled apples, such as Granny Smith or Rome

Rum Sauce

1/2 cup (1 stick) butter

3/4 cup packed brown sugar

1/4 cup cream

1/2 teaspoon rum extract, or 2 tablespoons rum

"In cooking, as in the arts, simplicity is a sign of perfection."
—*Curnonsky*

TURTLE CAKE

1 (18-ounce) package German
chocolate cake mix
1/2 cup evaporated milk
3/4 cup (1 1/2 sticks) margarine,
softened
1 (14-ounce) bag caramels
1/2 cup evaporated milk
1 1/4 cups chocolate chips
1 1/2 cups chopped pecans

Beat the cake mix, 1/2 cup evaporated milk and the margarine in a bowl until well blended. Spread half the batter in a 9×13-inch baking pan. Bake in a preheated 350-degree oven for 7 minutes.

Melt the caramels with 1/2 cup evaporated milk in the top of a double boiler over simmering water, stirring constantly. Pour the melted caramel mixture over the baked layer. Sprinkle evenly with the chocolate chips and pecans. Top with the remaining batter. Bake for 20 minutes.

MAKES 10 SERVINGS

The state tree of Texas, the pecan, dates back to prehistoric times. Its nut has a 70 percent fat content, which ranks highest of all nuts. This high fat content makes pecans more prone to rancidity. Stored in an airtight container, shelled pecans can be safely refrigerated for three months and frozen for six months.

HONEY BUN CAKE

For the cake, combine the cake mix, sour cream, eggs and oil in a bowl and mix well. Pour half the batter into a greased 9×13-inch cake pan or bundt pan. Combine the cinnamon and brown sugar in a small bowl and sprinkle over the cake batter. Pour in the remaining batter. (You may reserve a small amount of the topping to sprinkle over the top of the cake.) Bake in a preheated 350-degree oven for 40 minutes.

For the icing, combine the confectioners' sugar, milk and vanilla in a medium bowl. Mix until blended and of spreading consistency. Pour over the hot cake.

MAKES 10 TO 12 SERVINGS

Cake

1 (18-ounce) package yellow
   cake mix

1 cup sour cream

4 eggs

3/4 cup vegetable oil

1 tablespoon cinnamon

1 cup packed brown sugar

Quick Vanilla Icing

2 cups confectioners' sugar

1/4 cup milk

1 teaspoon vanilla extract

Marco Polo is credited with bringing the piñata to Italy from China. First used for religious holidays, paper mache piñatas are now used for various types of celebrations including birthdays, holidays such as Halloween, and Hispanic traditions such as Las Posadas. Piñatas can be filled with candy or prizes, or used for decoration.

153

SUNKEN GARDEN

*The original architect of San Antonio's Sunken Garden had the right recipe
for turning a utilitarian stone quarry into beautiful Japanese Gardens.
Rock from the quarry was used for the arched bridges and winding pathways
that connect quiet pools and gardens. During WWII, the original name was
changed from Japanese to Chinese. In 1984, the title "Japanese" was reinstated.*

QUICK TRES LECHES CAKE

Prepare the cake mix according to the package directions, baking in a bundt pan. Cool slightly and invert the pan to release the cake. Return the cake to the pan and poke holes all over the top.

Combine the sweetened condensed milk, half-and-half and evaporated milk in a blender container and process until blended. Pour the mixture over the cake in the pan. The mixture will soak up quickly. Chill, covered, for 4 hours or longer.

Invert the pan onto a serving platter. Let stand until the cake falls from the pan. Frost with the whipped topping and sprinkle with almonds .

MAKES 12 TO 16 SERVINGS

1 (18-ounce) package white cake mix
1 (14-ounce) can sweetened condensed milk
1 1/2 cups half-and-half
2 (5-ounce) cans evaporated milk
8 ounces whipped topping
Sliced almonds or toasted coconut

The United States Air Force has a strong presence in San Antonio. Randolph Air Force Base serves as a training center for flyers. Its Spanish Colonial Revival-style architecture has earned the title, "Showplace of the Air Force." Lackland Air Force Base is the entry processing station for recruit basic training. It is a common sight to see newly graduated trainees and their families enjoying San Antonio.

MANDARIN ORANGE CAKE

1 (18-ounce) package yellow
cake mix
4 eggs
1/2 cup vegetable oil
1 (11-ounce) can
mandarin oranges
1 (4-ounce) package vanilla
instant pudding mix
1 (15-ounce) can
crushed pineapple
8 ounces whipped topping

Combine the cake mix, eggs, oil and oranges in a bowl. Beat for 2 minutes. Pour the batter into three greased and floured 9-inch cake pans. Bake in a preheated 350-degree oven for 20 minutes. Cool completely. Combine the pudding mix, pineapple and whipped topping in a bowl and mix well, making sure the pudding mix is completely incorporated. Spread between the layers and over the top and side of the cake. Chill until ready to serve.

MAKES 10 TO 12 SERVINGS

MEXICAN WEDDING CAKE

2 cups all-purpose flour
2 cups sugar
1 teaspoon baking soda
1 teaspoon salt
1 (20-ounce) can crushed
pineapple in heavy syrup
2 eggs, lightly beaten
1 cup finely chopped pecans
8 ounces cream cheese, softened
1/2 cup (1 stick) butter, softened
2 cups confectioners' sugar
1 teaspoon vanilla extract

Mix the flour, sugar, baking soda and salt in a large bowl with a spoon. Add the pineapple, eggs and pecans and mix well with a spoon. Pour into two greased 9-inch cake pans. Bake in a preheated 350-degree oven for 30 minutes or until golden brown. Cool completely.

Beat the cream cheese and butter in a bowl until fluffy and well blended. Add the confectioners' sugar and vanilla and mix well. Spread between the layers and over the top and side of the cake.

MAKES 16 SERVINGS

PUMPKIN BUTTERSCOTCH CAKE

Combine the sugar and oil in a mixing bowl and beat until light and fluffy. Add the eggs and mix well. Add the flour, baking powder, baking soda, salt and cinnamon and beat until smooth. Add the pumpkin, pecans and butterscotch chips and mix well. Pour the batter into a greased and floured 9×13-inch cake pan. Bake in a preheated 350-degree oven for 40 minutes or until the cake springs back when lightly touched. Cool completely. Frost with your favorite frosting.

MAKES 18 TO 24 SERVINGS

2 cups sugar

1 cup vegetable oil

4 eggs

2 cups all-purpose flour

2 teaspoons baking powder

2 teaspoons baking soda

1/2 teaspoon salt

1 teaspoon cinnamon

2 cups canned pumpkin

1 cup chopped pecans

1 (11-ounce) package butterscotch chips

La Villita was first settled by Spanish soldiers serving at the Alamo. During the late 1800s, German and French settlers added new buildings for commercial purposes. Today La Villita is an area of shops and studios that features the work of local artists and craftsmen. La Villita hosts many San Antonio festivals such as Fiesta's "Night in Old San Antonio" (NIOSA). Its historic nondenominational church is the sight of many weddings.

BLUE RIBBON RED VELVET CAKE

Cake

1 cup (2 sticks) butter, softened

2 cups sugar

2 eggs

1 tablespoon vinegar

1 tablespoon baking cocoa

2^{1}/2 cups cake flour

^{1}/2 teaspoon salt

1^{1}/2 teaspoons baking soda

1 cup buttermilk

1 teaspoon vanilla extract

2 ounces red food coloring

Fluffy Coconut Walnut Frosting

1 cup evaporated milk

2 teaspoons all-purpose flour

1 cup granulated sugar

1 cup (2 sticks) butter, softened

1 cup chopped walnuts (optional)

1 cup coconut (optional)

1 teaspoon vanilla extract

Confectioners' sugar

For the cake, beat the butter and sugar in a bowl until light and fluffy. Add the eggs and mix well. Combine the vinegar and baking cocoa in a bowl, stirring to make a paste. Add to the egg mixture and mix well.

Sift together the flour, salt and baking soda. Add to the egg mixture alternately with the buttermilk, beating well after each addition. Beat in the vanilla and food coloring.

Pour the batter into two greased, wax paper-lined 8×8-inch cake pans. Bake in a preheated 350-degree oven for 35 minutes. Cool completely.

For the frosting, combine the milk and flour in a saucepan and blend until smooth. Cook over low heat until thickened, whisking constantly; cool.

Beat the butter and granulated sugar in a bowl until light and fluffy. Add to the flour mixture and mix well. Stir in the walnuts, coconut and vanilla. Add enough confectioners' sugar to make of a spreading consistency.

MAKES 12 SERVINGS

TOFFEE CRUNCH CAKE

Prepare and bake the cake mix according to the package directions, adding 1 teaspoon almond flavoring. Pour the sweetened condensed milk over the hot cake; cool. Chill, covered, in the refrigerator. Mix the whipped topping and 1 teaspoon almond flavoring in a bowl. Frost the cake. Sprinkle with the almonds and toffee bits, pressing them into the topping. Chill, covered, until ready to serve.

MAKES 15 SERVINGS

*1 (18-ounce) package white
 cake mix*
1 teaspoon almond extract
*1 (14-ounce) can sweetened
 condensed milk*
12 ounces whipped topping
1 teaspoon almond extract
1/2 cup toasted slivered almonds
1 cup crushed toffee bits

WAR CAKE

Mix the first eight ingredients in a saucepan. Bring to a boil. Cook for 3 minutes. Cool completely. Add a mixture of the baking soda, salt and warm water and mix well. Sift the flour and baking powder together and add to the batter; mix well. Stir in the pecans. Spoon into a floured greased tube pan. Bake in a preheated 325-degree oven for 1 1/2 hours.

MAKES 20 SERVINGS

2 cups packed brown sugar
2/3 cup shortening
2 cups water
1 1/2 cups raisins
1 1/2 cups golden raisins
2 teaspoons cinnamon
1 teaspoon ground cloves
1/2 teaspoon nutmeg
2 teaspoons baking soda
1 teaspoon salt
3 tablespoons warm water
4 cups all-purpose flour
1 teaspoon baking powder
2 cups chopped pecans

This cake was developed during World War I when milk, eggs and butter were in short supply. At the time it was known as Milkless, Eggless, Butterless Cake. In World War II, when those goods were again scarce, it became known as War Cake.

PARTONI SQUARES

2 cups crushed vanilla wafers,
chocolate wafers or
graham crackers
1 teaspoon almond extract or
vanilla extract
1/3 cup chopped toasted almonds
6 tablespoons butter, melted
1/2 gallon good-quality vanilla
ice cream, softened
1 (12-ounce) jar apricot or
other preserves

Combine the vanilla wafers, almond flavoring, almonds and butter in a medium bowl and mix well. Press half the mixture over the bottom of a buttered 9×9-inch or 9×13-inch pan. Layer with the ice cream, apricot preserves and remaining crumb mixture one-half at a time. Freeze until serving time. Cut into squares to serve. You may substitute pecans for the almonds.

MAKES 9 TO 12 SERVINGS

NAPOLEON CREMES

1/2 cup (1 stick) butter, softened
1/4 cup granulated sugar
1/4 cup baking cocoa
1 teaspoon vanilla extract
1 egg, lightly beaten
2 cups crushed graham crackers
1 cup flaked coconut
1/2 cup (1 stick) butter, softened
3 tablespoons milk
1 (4-ounce) package vanilla
instant pudding mix
2 cups confectioners' sugar
1 (6-ounce) package semisweet
chocolate chips
2 tablespoons butter

Mix 1/2 cup butter, the granulated sugar, baking cocoa and vanilla in the top of a double boiler over simmering water. Cook until the butter melts, stirring constantly. Add the egg and cook until thickened, stirring constantly. Stir in the graham cracker crumbs and coconut. Press into a 9×9-inch pan. Beat 1/2 cup butter in a bowl until fluffy. Add the next 3 ingredients and beat until fluffy. Spread evenly over the crust. Chill until firm. Melt the chocolate chips with 2 tablespoons butter in the top of a double boiler over simmering water and spread over pudding layer; chill slightly. Score the chocolate into 3/4×2-inch bars. Chill until firm. Cut into bars to serve.

MAKES ABOUT 44 BARS

AMARETTO CHUNK COOKIES

Mix the flour, baking soda, baking powder and salt in a bowl. Beat the next three ingredients in a bowl until fluffy. Beat in the eggs, liqueur and almond flavoring. Reduce the speed to low. Beat in the flour mixture just until blended. Stir in the remaining ingredients. Drop by heaping tablespoonfuls 2 inches apart onto ungreased cookie sheets. Bake in a preheated 375-degree oven for 10 to 12 minutes or until the edges are golden brown. Cool on wire racks. Store in an airtight container at room temperature for up to 1 week or freeze for up to 3 months.

MAKES 84 COOKIES

2 1/2 cups all-purpose flour
1 teaspoon baking soda
1 teaspoon baking powder
1/2 teaspoon salt
1 cup (2 sticks) butter, softened
1 cup packed brown sugar
1/2 cup granulated sugar
2 eggs
1 tablespoon amaretto
2 teaspoons almond extract
2 cups chocolate chips
1 cup flaked coconut
1 cup sliced almonds

LUSCIOUS APRICOT BARS

Simmer the apricots with water to cover in a saucepan for 10 minutes. Drain, cool and chop. Beat the butter, 1 cup flour and granulated sugar in a bowl until crumbly. Press into a greased 9×9-inch baking pan. Bake in a preheated 350-degree oven for 20 minutes. Sift together the next three ingredients. Beat the brown sugar and eggs in a bowl until fluffy. Stir in the flour mixture. Stir in the vanilla, pecans and apricots. Spread over the baked layer. Bake for 30 minutes or until cooked through. Cool in the pan. Cut into bars. Coat with confectioners' sugar.

MAKES 9 SERVINGS

2/3 cup dried apricots, rinsed
1/2 cup (1 stick) butter, softened
1 cup sifted all-purpose flour
1/4 cup granulated sugar
1/3 cup sifted all-purpose flour
1/2 teaspoon baking powder
1/4 teaspoon salt
1 cup packed brown sugar
2 eggs, beaten
1/2 teaspoon vanilla extract
1/2 to 3/4 cup chopped pecans
Confectioners' sugar

KICKOFF CHERRY-CHOCOLATE CHUNK COOKIES

1 cup (2 sticks) unsalted
butter, softened

3/4 cup shortening

1 1/2 cups granulated sugar

1 1/2 cups packed brown sugar

2 teaspoons salt

1 tablespoon vanilla extract

1 egg

1 egg white

2 tablespoons cold water

2 1/2 cups unbleached flour

2 1/2 cups rolled oats

1 teaspoon baking soda

2 cups walnuts, finely chopped

15 ounces semisweet baking
chocolate, cut into
medium chunks

8 ounces toffee bits

1 1/2 cups dried cherries or
sweetened cranberries

Beat the butter, shortening, granulated sugar and brown sugar in a bowl until light and fluffy. Add the salt, vanilla, egg and egg white and beat until fluffy. Add the water and mix well.

Combine the flour, oats and baking soda in a bowl and mix well. Add to the batter and mix just until combined. Stir in the walnuts, chocolate, toffee bits and cherries. Chill in the refrigerator until firm enough to handle.

Roll pieces of the dough into balls. Arrange on a parchment-lined cookie sheet and flatten each ball. Bake in a preheated 350-degree oven for 10 to 15 minutes or until set and brown at the edges. Cool slightly on the cookie sheet. Remove to a wire rack to cool completely.

MAKES 48 COOKIES

PRALINES

Combine the granulated sugar, brown sugar, corn syrup and cream in a saucepan and mix well. Bring to a boil and boil until the mixture reaches the soft ball stage (234 to 240 degrees). Add the pecans and bring almost to a boil. Remove from the heat and stir in the maple extract. Arrange sheets of waxed paper over paper towels on a work surface. Drop the candy mixture by spoonfuls onto the waxed paper. Cool completely. Store in an airtight container or wrap individually in plastic wrap.

2 cups granulated sugar
1 cup packed light brown sugar
3 tablespoons light corn syrup
1 cup whipping cream
4 cups pecans
2 teaspoons maple extract

MAKES ABOUT 60 PIECES

BUTTERMILK PRALINES

Combine the sugar, baking soda, buttermilk and corn syrup in a heavy saucepan and mix well. Cook over medium-high heat for 10 minutes or until the mixture reaches soft ball stage (234 to 240 degrees), stirring frequently as the mixture approaches 234 degrees. Remove from the heat and add the butter, vanilla and pecans and mix well. Cool for about 5 minutes. Stir until the candy begins to thicken. Drop by teaspoonfuls onto waxed paper or foil. Let cool completely.

2 cups sugar
1 teaspoon baking soda
1 cup buttermilk
2 tablespoons light corn syrup
1/4 cup (1/2 stick) butter
2 teaspoons vanilla extract
2 cups pecans

MAKES 24 TO 36 PIECES

*A gentle cruise down the placid San Antonio River is a relaxing
way to see the city from another point of view.*

RENOWNED RESTAURANTS, CELEBRITY CHEFS & CLEVER COOKS

OUR COMPLIMENTS TO SOME OF THE WONDERFUL CHEFS WHO "SERVE" SAN ANTONIO'S BEST-LOVED FOOD!

CHEF FOR ALL SEASONS
CATERING
Chef Stephen Shearer

CENTER FOR FOODS
OF THE AMERICAS
Chef Shelley Grieshaber
210-222-1113

CENTRAL MARKET
COOKING SCHOOL
Mary Martini
210-368-8600

CRUMPETS
Chef François Meader
210-821-5454

DRY COMAL CREEK
VINEYARD
Bonnie L. Houser
830-885-4121

GOURMET FOODS BY EVA
Eva O'Mahoney
210-655-0860

GUENTHER HOUSE
RESTAURANT
Chef Nancy Cato
210-227-1061

Phil Hardberger, Mayor
CITY OF SAN ANTONIO
2005–

LA PALOMA RIVER WALK
Chef Fernando Hernandez
210-212-0566

LA SCALA EUROPEAN
DINING
Chef Cesare Brambilla
210-366-1515

LEARN ABOARD!
Chef Michael H. Flores
210-545-2433

LOS BARRIOS MEXICAN
RESTAURANT
Diana Barrios Treviño
210-732-6017

PLAZA CLUB
Chef Dan Lewis
210-227-4191

SCENIC LOOP CAFE
Chef Beau Smith
210-687-1818

TEXAS FARM TO TABLE
Chefs Elise & Brian Montgomery
210-444-1404

THE LODGE RESTAURANT
Chef Jason Dady
210-349-8466

THE MELTING POT
Denise & DeWayne Faust
210-479-6358

"THE ULTIMATE COOKIE"
Christine Mose
cmose@satx.rr.com

ROASTED CORN POBLANO SOUP

Scenic Loop Café

1/4 cup vegetable oil

3 tablespoons butter

2 large yellow onions, chopped

12 garlic cloves, chopped

12 pounds frozen corn kernels

3 pounds tomatoes, crushed

12 quarts chicken broth

2 pounds roasted poblano chiles, chopped

2 tablespoons cumin

2 tablespoons pepper

12 ounces caldo de pollo

2 quarts half-and-half

Salt and pepper to taste

Heat the oil and butter in a large stockpot and sauté the onion and garlic until fragrant. Add the corn. Cook for 7 minutes. Add the tomatoes. Simmer for 5 minutes. Add the broth, poblano chiles, cumin, 2 tablespoons pepper and the caldo de pollo and mix well. Simmer but do not boil. Remove from the heat and add the half-and-half, salt and pepper to taste. Extra soup freezes well.

MAKES 12 QUARTS, ABOUT 96 SERVINGS

CURRIED ZUCCHINI SOUP

Dan Lewis, Plaza Club

3 tablespoons butter

1 1/2 cups diced yellow onions

12 cups chopped zucchini and/or yellow squash

1/2 tablespoon chopped garlic

1 tablespoon curry powder

1/4 cup all-purpose flour

10 cups chicken broth

Salt and pepper to taste

1 cup cream or half-and-half

Melt the butter in a stockpot over medium heat and sauté the onions until transparent. Add the zucchini and sauté for 5 minutes. Add the garlic, curry powder and flour and mix well. Stir in the broth. Simmer for 30 minutes, whisking frequently. Season with salt and pepper. Add the cream and heat through. You can substitute pumpkin for the zucchini.

MAKES 8 SERVINGS

TRADITIONAL SWISS CHEESE FONDUE

The Melting Pot

Combine the wine, garlic and lemon juice in the top of a double boiler over simmering water. Toss the cheese with the flour in a large bowl. Add the cheese in small amounts to the wine mixture. Heat until the mixture resembles warm honey, stirring constantly.

Pour the kirschwasser down the edges of the pan. (This helps the alcohol burn off.) Add five turns of the pepper grinder. Sprinkle with the nutmeg and mix well. Pour into a fondue pot for the table. Serve with fresh vegetables and bread.

MAKES 4 SERVINGS

1 cup white wine
1/2 teaspoon (rounded) minced garlic
Juice of 1/2 lemon
1 1/2 cups (6 ounces) grated Gruyère cheese
1 1/2 cups (6 ounces) shredded Emmentaler cheese
1 heaping teaspoon all-purpose flour
1 tablespoon kirschwasser (cherry brandy)
Freshly ground pepper
Pinch of grated nutmeg

CHICKEN IN CILANTRO SAUCE

Diana Barrios Trevino, Los Barrios Mexican Restaurant

6 boneless skinless chicken breasts
2 or 3 serrano chiles
2 (5-ounce) cans
evaporated milk
1 bunch cilantro, tough stems
removed and leaves
finely chopped
Salt and pepper to taste
2 tablespoons vegetable oil
1/4 onion, sliced

Combine the chicken and water to cover in a large pot. Cover and bring to a boil. Reduce the heat and simmer for 30 minutes. Drain well. Arrange on a serving platter and keep warm.

Combine the serrano chiles, evaporated milk, cilantro, salt and pepper in a blender. Process for 2 to 3 minutes until thoroughly combined.

Heat the oil in a medium saucepan over medium heat. Sauté the onion for 3 to 4 minutes until translucent. Add the cilantro mixture. Bring to a simmer. Reduce the heat and simmer gently for 10 minutes. Serve the sauce over the chicken.

MAKES 6 SERVINGS

RACK OF LAMB PROVENCAL

François Meader, Crumpets Restaurant and Bakery

2 tablespoons Dijon mustard
1 tablespoon chopped garlic
1 teaspoon salt
1 teaspoon pepper
1 tablespoon finely chopped
fresh rosemary
1 rack of lamb, cleaned, with
shank bone and top
fat removed

Combine the Dijon mustard, garlic, salt, pepper and rosemary in a small bowl. Brush the mixture over the lamb. Grill or broil or cook in a hot oven to medium-rare or medium.

MAKES 2 SERVINGS

DUCK CONFIT WITH ORECCHIETTE, CORN AND PARSLEY WITH TOASTED BREAD CRUMBS

Jason Dady, The Lodge Restaurant

Melt the fat in a large deep braising pan. Add the duck, making sure all the pieces are covered by the fat. Cover the pan with plastic wrap, then aluminum foil. Slow-roast in a preheated 250-degree oven for 6 to 8 hours. Remove from the oven and let cool. Remove the legs from the fat and pick the meat from the bones.

Pour the bread crumbs into a bowl. Process the olive oil and garlic in a food processor until well blended. Pour enough of the mixture into the bread crumbs to moisten them. Sprinkle 2 ounces Parmesan cheese into the bread crumb mixture and set aside.

Combine the pasta, cream, corn and duck confit in a large sauté pan. Bring to a boil. Cook until the cream is reduced by about one-fourth, or to the desired consistency. Stir in the parsley, kosher salt and pepper and mix well. Mound the pasta in a bowl. Top with the bread crumb mixture. Sprinkle additional Parmesan-Reggiano cheese on top.

Rotisserie chicken can be substituted.

MAKES 8 SERVINGS

1 gallon rendered duck fat

6 duck legs

4 ounces toasted garlic sourdough bread crumbs

1 cup extra-virgin olive oil

1 ounce chopped garlic

2 ounces grated Parmesan cheese

8 ounces orecchiette pasta, cooked to al dente and drained

1 quart heavy cream

2 ears corn, kernels cut off

1 bunch Italian parsley, chopped

Kosher salt and cracked black pepper to taste

Grated Parmesan-Reggiano cheese

SUCCULENT BRAISED LAMB SHANKS OR BEEF SHORT RIBS

Shelley Grieshaber, CIA

6 (1¹/4- to 1¹/2-pound) lamb
shanks, frenched, or 6 pounds
beef short ribs, trimmed
Coarse salt and freshly ground
pepper to taste
¹/2 cup olive oil
2 ribs celery, coarsely chopped
1 carrot, coarsely chopped
1 large yellow onion,
coarsely chopped
3 tablespoons olive oil
¹/2 cup tomato paste
5 sprigs fresh thyme
1 bay leaf
1 tablespoon peppercorns
3 anchovy fillets
1 garlic head, cut into halves
2 cups dry red wine
¹/3 cup white vinegar
1 teaspoon sugar
2 cups beef broth
2 cups chicken broth

Season the lamb shanks with coarse salt and pepper. Brown the shanks all over in ¹/2 cup olive oil in a skillet over medium-high heat. Arrange in a roasting pan. Sauté the celery, carrot and onion in 3 tablespoons olive oil in a large pan over medium-high heat for 8 to 10 minutes or until tender. Add the tomato paste and cook for 1 to 2 minutes. Stir in the thyme, bay leaf, peppercorns, anchovies and garlic and cook for 2 to 3 minutes. Stir in the wine, vinegar and sugar. Bring to a boil over high heat. Reduce the heat to medium. Add the beef broth and chicken broth and bring to a simmer. Pour over the shanks. Bake, covered, in a preheated 325-degree oven for 1 hour. Uncover and bake for 3 hours longer or until very tender, turning the shanks every 30 minutes. Arrange on a serving platter. Strain the cooking liquid, discarding the solids. Skim the fat. Stir in hot water to thin the sauce, if desired. Serve with the lamb shanks.

MAKES 6 SERVINGS

Whether you're a beef eater or a lamb lover, this simple, succulent, fall-off-the-bone recipe is perfect for do-ahead parties or a quiet Sunday supper. All it needs is mashed potatoes plain or flavored with horseradish, roasted garlic, or Parmesan cheese. Soft, creamy polenta or a ragout of white beans is a great side dish option with a twist.

BRAISED BEEF WITH CABERNET AND BRANDY

Bonnie L. Houser, Dry Comal Creek Vineyards

Fry the bacon until cooked through but not crisp. Drain, pat dry and coarsely chop.

Melt the butter in a heavy pan. Brown the meat well on all sides. Add the brandy. Simmer, covered, over low heat for 30 minutes. Add the bacon, onions, warm water, garlic, bouquet garni, salt and pepper. Add 1 cup of the wine. Bake in a preheated 300-degree oven for 2 hours, adding more brandy and wine if needed to prevent the pan from cooking dry. Add the mushrooms and olives. Bake for 30 minutes longer. Serve with rice, noodles or potatoes.

MAKES 6 TO 8 SERVINGS

4 slices bacon

2 to 4 tablespoons butter

2 1/2 pounds beef rump or round

3/4 to 1 cup brandy

8 to 10 small whole onions

1 1/2 cups warm water

2 garlic cloves

1 to 2 teaspoons bouquet garni

Salt and pepper to taste

1/2 cup Dry Comal Creek
    Vineyards Cabernet
    Sauvignon

8 to 12 mushrooms

12 pitted green olives, blanched

This dish is a favorite adapted from the Samuel Chamberlain Calendar of French Cooking, 1962. Serve with Dry Comal Creek Vineyards Merlot, Cabernet Sauvignon, or Black Spanish.

FILETE GUAJILLO

Fernando Hernandez, La Paloma River Walk

Guajillo Sauce

1 pound guajillo chiles,
stems removed
1 white onion
3 garlic cloves
2 pounds Roma tomatoes
1 cup tomato paste
1 teaspoon salt
1 teaspoon pepper
3/4 cup vegetable oil
2 quarts water
Salt and pepper to taste

Beef

12 (4-ounce) beef medallions
Pinch each of salt and pepper
1/2 cup vegetable oil
Sliced white mushrooms
Mozzarella cheese to taste

For the sauce, process the guajillo chiles, onion, garlic, tomatoes, tomato paste, 1 teaspoon salt, 1 teaspoon pepper, oil and water in a blender until puréed. Pour through a strainer and discard the solids. Pour into a 3-quart pan. Season with salt and pepper to taste. Bring to a boil over medium-high heat and cook for 15 minutes. Reduce the heat and cook, stirring, until the sauce begins to thicken. Remove from the heat and set aside.

For the beef, season the medallions with salt and pepper. Heat the oil in a skillet and brown the medallions and mushrooms. Cook for 5 minutes or to the desired degree of doneness. Cover an ovenproof plate with guajillo sauce. Top with two beef medallions in the center. Cover with the mushrooms and juices from the skillet. Sprinkle with cheese. Place under the broiler for 2 minutes to melt.

MAKES 6 SERVINGS

Located in a historic limestone building on the San Antonio River, La Paloma River Walk takes pride in serving authentic Continental Mexican Cuisine. Owned and operated by the Roger A. Flores family for over 25 years, the decor of this eclectic bistro-style restaurant features original artwork by its owners and artists Evangelina and Roger O. Flores. La Paloma's Executive Chef Fernando Hernandez's philosophy is to cook with joy and to put the passion for his art into every dish.

LEMONY GOAT CHEESE DRESSING

Texas Farm to Table Café

Combine the goat cheese, lemon zest, lemon juice and enough half-and-half to create a pourable consistency in a blender or food processor. Process until well blended. Season lightly with salt and generously with pepper.

MAKES ABOUT 2 CUPS

3 logs goat cheese
Zest and juice of 2 or 3 lemons
Half-and-half
Salt and pepper to taste

TEJAS CAESAR DRESSING

Texas Farm to Table Café

Coat the serrano chiles with a small amount of vegetable oil. Roast, grill or broil until the skins blacken slightly. Place in a paper bag and close the top. Let stand for 15 minutes. Remove the skins and seeds.

Combine the serrano chiles, egg yolks, cheese, water, olive oil, anchovies, cilantro, garlic, shallots, salt and pepper in a blender or food processor. Process until well blended.

MAKES ABOUT 3 CUPS

3 serrano chiles
Vegetable oil
2 egg yolks
1 cup crumbled cotija cheese
1 cup water
1 cup olive oil
4 anchovies
1/2 bunch cilantro
3 garlic cloves
1 shallot
Salt and pepper to taste

CHICKEN SALAD

Texas Farm to Table Café

5 ribs celery
12 dill pickles
8 (6-ounce) chicken breasts,
cooked and chopped
1 cup mayonnaise
Paprika
Pinch of cayenne pepper
Salt and pepper to taste

Chop the celery and pickles. Combine in a bowl with the chicken and mayonnaise. Add enough paprika to lightly color the mixture. Add the cayenne pepper, salt and pepper and mix well.

MAKES 8 TO 10 SERVINGS

SAUERBRATEN

Phil Hardberger, Mayor of San Antonio

1 large brisket, trimmed
1 1/2 cups red wine vinegar
1 cup red wine
1 bay leaf
1/2 teaspoon thyme
3 garlic cloves, minced
3 peppercorns
1 allspice berry
All-purpose flour for coating
2 garlic cloves, minced
1 onion, sliced
1/2 cup vegetable oil
1/4 cup (1/2 stick) butter
1 to 2 tablespoons all-purpose flour
1 1/2 cups sour cream

Mix the red wine vinegar, red wine, bay leaf, thyme, three minced garlic cloves, peppercorns and allspice in a large bowl or plastic bag. Add the brisket and refrigerate for four days, turning once a day. Remove the meat from the marinade and pat dry. Coat with flour. Heat the oil and butter in a Dutch oven. Brown the brisket on all sides. Strain the marinade into the Dutch oven, discarding the solids. Add the onion and 2 minced garlic cloves. Roast in a preheated 250-degree oven for 4 hours. Remove from the oven. Arrange the brisket on a platter and keep hot. Thicken the pan gravy with 1 to 2 tablespoons flour. Cook over low heat, stirring to break up any lumps. Add the sour cream and heat through. Serve over sliced brisket.

MAKES 8 TO 10 SERVINGS

VEAL MOUTARDE

Cesare Brambilla, La Scala

Sprinkle the veal with seasoned salt. Spread the flour on a plate or waxed paper. Coat the veal with the flour, shaking off any excess. Heat the oil in a large skillet. Sauté the green onions and move to the side of the pan. Add the veal in a single layer. Brown on one side and turn. Add the wine and Dijon mustard and mix well. Cook for 1 to 2 minutes longer or until brown on both sides. Remove the veal from the skillet to a warm platter. Cook until the liquid is reduced by two-thirds. Add the cream and cook until thickened to the desired consistency, stirring and scraping up the brown bits. Spoon the sauce over the veal and serve.

MAKES 2 SERVINGS

8 ounces veal scallopini, cut 1/4-inch thick and pounded to a 1/8-inch thickness
Seasoned salt (or salt and pepper) to tatse
All-purpose flour for coating
1 1/2 tablespoons vegetable oil
1 cup chopped green onions
1/2 cup white wine
1 to 2 tablespoons Dijon mustard
1/3 cup cream

CILANTRO SHRIMP

Michael H. Flores, CIA, Learn Aboard!

Combine the green onions, cilantro, lime juice, garlic, corn oil, sugar, serrano chiles and salt in a blender. Process until well-blended. Pour the mixture over the shimp in a bowl. Cover and refrigerate for 8 to 12 hours. Serve as an appetizer or first course.

MAKES 6 TO 10 SERVINGS

5 green onions
1 bunch cilantro, washed
1 cup freshly squeezed lime juice
3 garlic cloves
2 tablespoons corn oil
3 tablespoons sugar
2 serrano chiles, stems removed
1 tablespoon kosher salt
2 pounds shrimp, cooked, peeled and tails left on

PINON-CRUSTED SALMON ATOP A TORTILLA SALAD

Michael H. Flores, CIA, Learn Aboard!

5 ounces pine nuts (piñon)

1 teaspoon salt

1 teaspoon pepper

1 teaspoon ground coriander

1/4 cup (1/2 stick) butter, softened

2 pounds boneless skinless salmon fillets

5 to 7 corn tortillas

1/2 cup corn oil

2 tomatoes, chopped

1/4 cup sliced green onions

1 or 2 jalapeño chiles, minced

1/2 cup cilantro leaves

Juice of 2 limes (about 1/4 cup)

2 avocados, chopped

1/2 cup fresh or frozen corn kernels

1/2 cup rinsed cooked black beans

2 teaspoons salt

1/2 teaspoon cumin

1 teaspoon chile powder

Combine the pine nuts, 1 teaspoon salt, pepper, coriander and butter in a blender and process until well blended. Spread over the salmon. Bake in a preheated 350-degree oven for 20 minutes.

Cut the tortillas into halves, then into 1/2- to 1/4-inch strips. Fry the strips in the hot corn oil for about 3 minutes or until crisp. Drain on paper towels and cool.

Combine the tortilla strips, tomatoes, green onions, jalapeño chiles, cilantro, lime juice, avocados, corn, black beans, 2 teaspoons salt, cumin and chile powder in a large bowl and mix gently. Spread on individual plates or a serving platter and top with the salmon.

MAKES 5 SERVINGS

Hailed as a "San Antonio phenomenon," Michael Flores has gained national recognition for his unique culinary creations. Flores launched "Learn Aboard," a cooking class on a barge on the San Antonio River, where he prepares cuisine which relies on traditional methods of classical cuisine while incorporating ingredients that mirror an appreciation of people and their diverse cultures.

TAMARIND-CURED BEEF TENDERLOIN WITH A GORGONZOLA PUMPKIN SEED SALSA

Michael H. Flores, CIA, Learn Aboard!

For the beef tenderloins, combine the fillets, tamarind base, tequila, corn oil, serrano chile and garlic in an extra-large sealable plastic bag. Squeeze out the air and seal. Refrigerate for 24 hours, turning occasionally to coat.

For the salsa, combine the pumpkin seeds, vinegar, green onions, cheese, olive oil, cilantro, jalapeño chile, garlic and lime juice in a bowl. Season with salt. Refrigerate for at least 8 hours. The flavor is very different before and after refrigeration.

Heat corn oil in a large skillet. Remove the fillets from the marinade, discarding the marinade. Season with salt and pepper. Sear in hot corn oil for 3 minutes on each side. Watch carefully, as the marinade can burn. Arrange on a roasting pan and finish in a preheated 350-degree oven for 4 to 10 minutes. Top with the salsa to serve.

MAKES 4 TO 6 SERVINGS

Princesa Tamarind Beverage Base is available at Latin American markets.

Beef Tenderloins and Marinade

4 to 6 (6-ounce) beef tenderloin fillets

1 (16-ounce) bottle of Princesa Tamarind Beverage Base

1/4 cup tequila

1/4 cup corn oil

1 serrano chile, coarsely chopped

1 garlic clove, crushed

Salsa

1 cup pumpkin seeds, toasted

3 tablespoons sherry vinegar

2 green onions, sliced

4 ounces Gorgonzola cheese, crumbled

2 tablespoons olive oil

1 large handful cilantro, chopped

1 jalapeño chile, seeded and minced

1/2 teaspoon minced garlic

Juice of 1 lime

Salt to taste

Corn oil for sautéing

Pepper to taste

SHRIMP A LA MITLA

Roger Flores, La Paloma River Walk

3 garlic cloves, chopped
1/3 stick butter, melted
1 pound large shrimp, peeled
and deveined
8 ounces tomatillos
1/4 onion, chopped
1 tomato, chopped
2 serrano chiles, minced
4 sprigs cilantro, minced
1/4 teaspoon salt, or to taste
Juice of 1/2 lime or lemon

Sauté the garlic in the butter in a saucepan over medium heat. Add the shrimp. Cook until pink on one side, and then turn.

Combine the tomatillos and water to cover in a saucepan. Bring to a simmer and cook for 10 minutes; drain. Process the tomatillos in a blender until smooth.

Combine the onion, tomato, serrano chiles and cilantro in a bowl and mix well. Add to the skillet. Cook until the onion begins to soften. Add the tomatillo sauce, salt and lime juice. Bring to a boil. Reduce the heat and cook for 1 minute. Serve hot garnished with lemon or lime slices and fresh cilantro sprigs. Serve with saffron rice or Spanish rice and black beans.

MAKES 4 SERVINGS

CHEESE STRUDEL

Eva O'Mahoney, Gourmet Foods by Eva

For the pastry, combine the butter, egg yolks, sugar, milk, baking powder, vanilla and 1¹/2 cups of the flour and mix well to form a dough. Knead the remaining ¹/2 cup flour into the dough. Let the dough rest for 15 minutes.

For the filling and topping, combine the cream cheese, cottage cheese, sugar, butter, vanilla and raisins in a bowl and beat until well blended.

Cut the dough into halves. Roll out each half into a rectangle. Spread each rectangle with the cheese filling. Fold the long sides over the filling to the center. Roll to enclose. Arrange seam side up on a baking sheet. The strudel will open while baking to show the filling.

Brush with a mixture of the egg and milk. Bake in a preheated 325-degree oven for 25 minutes or until brown. Sprinkle the hot strudel with confectioners' sugar. Cut into slices to serve.

MAKES 12 TO 15 SERVINGS

Strudel Pastry

6 tablespoons butter

3 egg yolks

¹/4 cup sugar

¹/4 cup milk

1 teaspoon baking powder

¹/2 teaspoon vanilla extract

2 cups all-purpose flour

Filling and Topping

4 ounces cream cheese

1 cup dry curd cottage cheese

¹/2 cup sugar

2 tablespoons butter, melted

¹/2 teaspoon vanilla extract

¹/2 cup raisins

1 egg, beaten

Milk

Confectioners' sugar

EGGPLANT CASSEROLE

Mary Martini, Central Market

Cheese and Egg Cream Sauce

3 eggs

3/4 cup (3 ounces) grated
Parmigiano-Reggiano cheese

1/2 cup heavy cream

Béchamel Sauce

1 tablespoon flour

1 cup milk

1 cup heavy cream

Salt and pepper to taste

Nutmeg to taste

Eggplant

2 1/2 pounds eggplant,
cut into 1/4-inch slices

Salt to taste

2 cups flour

2 cups olive oil

6 ounces fontina cheese,
thinly sliced or grated

3 cups tomato sauce

1/4 cup (1 ounce) grated
Parmigiano-Reggiano cheese

For the cream sauce, combine the eggs, cheese and cream. Cover and set aside.

For the béchamel sauce, whisk the flour with 1/4 cup of the milk in a saucepan until smooth. Stir in the remaining milk and cream. Cook over medium heat for 5 minutes or until thick, stirring constantly. Cool and season with salt, pepper and nutmeg.

For the eggplant, sprinkle the eggplant with the salt and sweat for 2 to 4 hours; rinse and pat dry. Coat with the flour. Fry in the olive oil in a skillet until golden; drain on paper towels. Spread a thin layer of béchamel sauce over the bottom of a greased baking dish. Layer half the eggplant, fontina cheese, tomato sauce and béchamel sauce in the prepared dish. Layer the remaining eggplant, fontina cheese, cream sauce, tomato sauce and béchamel sauce over the top. Sprinkle with the Parmigiano-Reggiano cheese. Bake in a preheated 350-degree oven for 35 to 40 minutes.

MAKES 8 SERVINGS

A fourth generation restaurateur, Mary Martini gained immeasurable experience working with and cooking beside her parents and brothers, who own and operate two restaurants in upper New York State. Central Market selected Martini to serve as Manager/Chef of the San Antonio Cooking School in 2001. Martini currently serves as a Board Member of the San Antonio Les Dames d'Escoffier.

WHOLE WHEAT APPLE PANCAKES

Stephen Shearer, CIA

Combine the flour, brown sugar, cornmeal, baking powder, baking soda, salt and cinnamon in a bowl. Beat the eggs, buttermilk and 3 tablespoons butter in a medium bowl. Pour into the flour mixture and mix just until moistened; do not overmix.

Pour 1/4 cup batter for each pancake onto a griddle or a skillet on medium-low to medium heat. Top with a layer of apples. Sprinkle with brown sugar. Add a small pat of butter. When the bottom of the pancake is brown, turn it over so the apples can caramelize. Serve apple side up.

MAKES 6 SERVINGS

1/2 cup all-purpose flour
1/2 cup whole wheat flour
1 tablespoon brown sugar
2 tablespoons cornmeal
1 teaspoon baking powder
1/4 teaspoon baking soda
1/2 teaspoon salt
1 tablespoon cinnamon
1 egg
1 cup buttermilk
3 tablespoons butter, melted, or
  3 tablespoons canola oil
2 apples, cored and cut into
  thin slices
Brown sugar for sprinkling
Butter or canola oil for cooking

BLUEBERRY SCONES

Christine Mose, The Ultimate Cookie

4 cups unsifted all-purpose flour
2 tablespoons sugar
4 teaspoons baking powder
1/2 teaspoon salt
1/2 teaspoon cream of tartar
3/4 cup (1 1/2 sticks) butter, chilled
1 egg yolk, beaten
1 1/2 cups half-and-half
1 1/2 cups fresh blueberries
1 egg white
1 tablespoon sugar

Combine the flour, 2 tablespoons sugar, the baking powder, salt and cream of tartar in a large bowl. Cut in the butter with a pastry blender or two knives until the mixture resembles coarse crumbs.

Stir the egg yolk and half-and-half together in a bowl. Add to the dry ingredients and mix lightly with a fork just until the mixture holds together and forms a soft dough.

Knead the dough on a lightly floured surface 5 or 6 times. Gently knead in the blueberries. Divide the dough into halves. Roll each half of the dough into a 7-inch round. Cut into four wedges each.

Place the scones 1 inch apart on a greased baking sheet. Prick the tops with a fork. Brush with the egg white and sprinkle with 1 tablespoon sugar. Bake in a preheated 425-degree oven for 15 to 18 minutes until golden brown. Serve warm.

MAKES 8 SERVINGS

*Scones are thought to be of Scottish origin.
Earlier scones were made into large round shapes that
were scored into triangles before baking.*

CREME BRULEE WITH RASPBERRY COULIS

Mary Martini and David Holtzman, Central Market Cooking School

For the raspberry coulis, process the raspberries, sugar and jam in a food processor until well blended. Pour through a fine sieve, discarding the solids. Pour 1/2 inch of coulis into each ramekin. Freeze until the coulis is hard.

Arrange six 1/2-cup ramekins on a double thickness of paper towels in a baking pan.

For the crème brûlée, beat the egg yolks until thickened. Add the sugar and beat until the sugar is dissolved and the mixture is light in color. Whisk in the cream and vanilla. Pour over the frozen raspberry coulis in the ramekins. Place the baking pan in the oven and pour in enough hot water to come halfway up the sides of the ramekins. Bake in a preheated 300-degree oven for 30 to 40 minutes or until the custards are set. Cool, and then chill for at least 2 hours. Spread 1/4 cup sugar evenly on top of the custards. Broil or use a kitchen torch until the sugar is light brown.

MAKES 6 SERVINGS

Raspberry Coulis
1 (12-ounce) bag frozen unsweetened raspberries, thawed
1/4 cup sugar
2 tablespoons raspberry jam

Crème Brûlée
6 egg yolks
6 tablespoons sugar
1 1/2 cups heavy cream
1 teaspoon vanilla
1/4 cup sugar

CONTRIBUTORS

Lenore Allred
Jeanne Anderson
Jacqueline Angert
Linda Armstrong
Joyce Arnold
Jeanette Atkinson
Ruby Bainum
Corie Barlow
Sandy Baumann
Barbara Bertolett
Rebecca Bogan
Mary Alice Bond
Colleen Boone
Martha Bowden
Sandy Boyd
Carole Ann Braden
Carol Bray
Suzanne Brown
Maria Esthela Buentello
Barbara Burleson
Brent Byers
Elaine Byers
Erin Byers
Melina Byers
Donna Campbell
Margo Chapman
Carolyn Clark
Pat Coleman
Carol Collins
Karen Crane
Patty Davis
Colleen Dement
Maye Dix
Rosemary Doyle
Shari Dybdahl
Linda Ellis
Jean Ferrari
Bette Flindell
Dixie Flory
Norma Floyd
Tina Freeborn
Joyce Gallegos
Ginny Glass
Cissi Glendening
June Gonzalez
Carolyn Grine
Barbara Haley
Betty Hans
Suzanne Harrison
Nancy Haugen

Betty Sue Hayes
Dolly Ann Hayes
Jo Herbold
Eunise Hermes
JoAnn Hickey
Doris Hill
Stephanie Hobbs
Peggy Foster Hooks
Billie-Kite Howlett
Leslie Huddleston
Carolyn Jaco
Sally James
Marsha Jernigan
Christy Johnston
Kay Lynn Johnston
K Joseph
Sybil Judge
Jean Karren
Jean T. Kendall
Georgia Khym-Heath
Mary Kilgore
Mary Kittle
Yvonne Kohutek
Carol Lapp
Marcia Lehman
Diane Leininger
Anita Lindner
Kevin Loop
Marilyn Loop
Cindy Manzotti
Julie Marshall
Gene Martin
Jennie Martin
Keene Martin
Helen McCrae
Sandy McDonald
Elsie McTee
Ruth Meador
Dorothy Mercer
Pat Meyers
Arlene Miller
Betty Neal
Joann Neal
Ginger Nicholas
Lenora Norton
Audrey Oetting
Marge Ognibene
Sherry Olberding
Judy Perry
Ruby Pesek

Carmen Pettit
Dianne Pool
Joan Porter
Betty Pruitt
Joyce Pruitt
Jan Ramert
Jimmy and Erin Ramert
Susan Ramirez
Virna Reposa
Ellie Richardson
Beth Roten
Janet B. Rund
Mary Russell
Deborah Sandheinrich
Marie Schmutz
Jonnie Schulz
Jane Sperber
Becky Staglik
Brenda Staglik
Sue Staglik
Mary Stephenson
Sammie Stevenson
Betty Storrs
Kathy Stull
Shirley Sweigart
Margaret Tarleton
LaRue Terry
Clayton Thompson, Jr.
Cheryl Tomandl
Betty Touchon
Stephanie Trede
Rachel Upson
Becky Walker
Beverly Wallace
Georgie Walters
Joan Weart
Sheila Webb
Nora Wheatly
Kari Willenbring
Freddie Williams
Monzita Williams
Virginia Williamson
Gene Willis
Carole Wilson
Norma Winchester
Alyne Woodring
Dorothy Woods
Pat Younts

INDEX

185

SERVING

San Antonio

A COOKBOOK FROM

ASSISTANCE LEAGUE® OF SAN ANTONIO

P.O. Box 13130
San Antonio, Texas 78213-0130
Phone (210) 732-1200
Fax (210) 732-1548
www.alsantonio.org
www.servingsanantoniocookbook.com

YOUR ORDER	QUANTITY	TOTAL
Serving San Antonio at $24.95 per book		$
Texas residents add 8.25% sales tax		$
Postage and handling at $7.00 for the first book; $3.00 for each additional book to the same address; $20.00 per case		$
	TOTAL	$

Name

Address

City   State   Zip

Telephone   Email

Method of Payment: [   ]   MasterCard   [   ] VISA

[   ]   Check payable to ASSISTANCE LEAGUE of San Antonio—Cookbook

Account Number   Expiration Date

Signature

Photocopies will be accepted.